A Nation at Risk

A Nation at Risk

The Full Account

The National Commission On Excellence in Education

Edited and Published by USA Research, Inc.
Portland, Oregon

The publisher wishes to acknowledge with gratitude the cooperation of the National Commission on Excellence in Education in assembling the text of the Commission's original report along with indispensable coverage of supporting research and hearing testimony.

Inquiries regarding this publication should be addressed to:

USA Research, Inc.
4380 SW Macadam Avenue
Portland, OR 97201-6406
telephone 503-274-6200
facsimile 503-274-6265

Library of Congress Catalog Card Number 84-50556
ISBN 0-917191-02-1 (paper)

Printed in the United States of America
Courier Companies, Inc.
Westford, Massachusetts

Typeface: Century Old Style

Published March, 1984
Second Printing July, 1992
Third Printing February, 1994

10   9   8   7   6   5   4   3

Table of Contents

List of Exhibits

Acknowledgements

To the public-minded citizens who took the trouble to share their concerns with us — frequently at their own expense in time, money, and effort — we extend our thanks. In all cases, we have benefited from their advice and taken their views into account; how we have treated their suggestions is, of course, our responsibility alone. In addition, we are grateful to the individuals in schools, universities, foundations, business, government, and communities throughout the United States who provided the facilities and staff so necessary to the success of our many public functions.

The Commission was impressed during the course of its activities by the diversity of opinion it received regarding the condition of American education and by conflicting views about what should be done. In many ways, the membership of the Commission itself reflected that diversity and difference of opinion during the course of its work. This report, nevertheless, gives evidence that men and women of good will can agree on common goals and on ways to pursue them.

We want to express particular appreciation to the Commission staff which, under the leadership of Executive Director Milton Goldberg, assisted us in our work and helped prepare this report. The staff included:

      Betty S. Baten
      Stella Carol Foley
      Peter H. Gerber
      James Harvey
      Arnetta D. LaGrone
      Alisa M. Longworth
      Mollie Shannahan MacAdams
      Penny S. McDonald
      Shelia L. Sam
      Haroldie K. Spriggs
      Tommy M. Tomlinson
      Susan Traiman
      Patricia A. Welch

Others who assisted us at various times throughout the course of our work include: Clifford Adelman, Ned Chalker, Cheryl Chase, Antoine M. Garibaldi, Charlesetta Griffin, Bruce Haslam, Carolyn Johnson, Sharon Jones, Lily A. Kliot, Andrew M. Lebby, Beverly Lindsay, Carolyn Lowe, Irene Lykes, Claude Mayberry, John M. Mays, Brad Mitchell, Jean Narayanan, Lewis Pike, John Ridgway, Joanne Saunders, Ramsay Selden, Gary Sykes, Marilyn A. Tapscott, and Douglas Wright. Also, the Commission owes a considerable debt to Editorial Experts, Inc. and Morgan-Bruchette Associates, both of Alexandria, Virginia, and in particular to Bruce Boston, Karen Burchette, Lee Mickle, and Ian McNett, for invaluable assistance in designing, editing, and producing this volume.

Finally, we sincerely appreciate the support and cooperation provided by Mary Jean LeTendre, Special Assistant to Secretary Bell; Donald J. Senese, Assistant Secretary, Office of Educational Research and Improvement; and Manuel J. Justiz, Director of the National Institute of Education.

Chapter 1
The Mission

Secretary of Education T. H. Bell created the National Commission on Excellence in Education on August 26, 1981, directing it to examine the quality of education in the United States and to make a report to the Nation and to him within 18 months of its first meeting. In accordance with the Secretary's instructions, this report contains practical recommendations for educational improvement and fulfills the Commission's responsibilities under the terms of its charter.

The Commission was created as a result of the Secretary's concern about "the widespread public perception that something is seriously remiss in our educational system." Soliciting the "support of all who care about our future," the Secretary noted that he was establishing the Commission based on his "responsibility to provide leadership, constructive criticism, and effective assistance to schools and universities."

The Commission's charter contained several specific charges to which we have given particular attention. These included:

■ assessing the quality of teaching and learning in our Nation's public and private schools, colleges, and universities;

■ comparing American schools and colleges with those of other advanced nations;

■ studying the relationship between college admissions requirements and student achievement in high school;

■ identifying educational programs which result in notable student success in college;

■ assessing the degree to which major social and educational changes in the last quarter century have affected student achievement; and

■ defining problems which must be faced and overcome if we are successfully to pursue the course of excellence in education.

The Commission's charter directed it to pay particular attention to teenage youth, and we have done so largely by focusing on high schools. Selective attention was given to the formative years spent in elementary schools, to higher education, and to vocational and technical programs. We refer those interested in the need for similar reform in higher education to the recent report of the American Council on Education, *To Strengthen the Quality of Higher Education.*

In going about its work the Commission has relied in the main upon five sources of information:

○ papers commissioned from experts on a variety of educational issues;

○ administrators, teachers, students, representatives of professional and public groups, parents, business leaders, public officials, and scholars who testified at eight meetings of the full Commission, six public hearings, two panel discussions, a symposium, and a series of meetings organized by the Department of Education's Regional Offices;

○ existing analyses of problems in education;

○ letters from concerned citizens, teachers, and administrators who volunteered extensive comments on problems and possibilities in American education; and

○ descriptions of notable programs and promising approaches in education.

To these public-minded citizens who took the trouble to share their concerns with us—frequently at their own expense in time, money, and effort—we extend our thanks. In all cases, we have benefited from their advice and taken their views into account; how we have treated their suggestions is, of course, our responsibility alone. In addition, we are grateful to the individuals in schools, universities, foundations, business, government, and communities throughout the United States who provided the facilities and staff so necessary to the success of our many public functions.

The Commission was impressed during the course of its activities by the diversity of opinion it received regarding the condition of American education and by conflicting views about what should be done. In many ways, the membership of the Commission itself reflected that diversity and difference of opinion during the course of its work. This report, nevertheless, gives evidence that men and women of good will can agree on common goals and on ways to pursue them.

The Commission's charter, the authors and topics of commissioned papers, a list of the public events, and a roster of the Commission's staff are included in the appendices which complete this volume.

Chapter 2
A Nation at Risk

Our Nation is at risk. Our once unchallenged preeminence in commerce, industry, science, and technological innovation is being overtaken by competitors throughout the world. This report is concerned with only one of the many causes and dimensions of the problem, but it is the one that undergirds American prosperity, security, and civility. We report to the American people that while we can take justifiable pride in what our schools and colleges have historically accomplished and contributed to the United States and the well-being of its people, the educational foundations of our society are presently being eroded by a rising tide of mediocrity that threatens our very future as a Nation and a people. What was unimaginable a generation ago has begun to occur—others are matching and surpassing our educational attainments.

If an unfriendly foreign power had attempted to impose on America the mediocre educational performance that exists today, we might well have viewed it as an act of war. As it stands, we have allowed this to happen to ourselves. We have even squandered the gains in student achievement made in the wake of the Sputnik challenge. Moreover, we have dismantled essential support systems which helped make those gains possible. We have, in effect, been committing an act of unthinking, unilateral educational disarmament.

Our society and its educational institutions seem to have lost sight of the basic purposes of schooling, and of the high expectations and disciplined effort needed to attain them. This report, the result of 18 months of study, seeks to generate reform of our educational system in fundamental ways and to renew the Nation's commitment to schools and colleges of high quality throughout the length and breadth of our land.

That we have compromised this commitment is, upon reflection, hardly surprising, given the multitude of often conflicting demands we have placed on our Nation's schools and colleges. They are routinely called on to provide solutions to personal, social, and political problems that the home and other institutions either will not or cannot resolve. We must understand that these demands on our schools and colleges often exact an educational cost as well as a financial one.

On the occasion of the Commission's first meeting, President Reagan noted the central importance of education in American life when he said: "Certainly there are few areas of American life as important to our society, to our people, and to our families as our schools and colleges." This report, therefore, is as much an open letter to the American people as it is a report to the Secretary of Education. We are confident that the American people, properly informed, will do what is right for their children and for the generations to come.

The Risk

History is not kind to idlers. The time is long past when America's destiny was assured simply by an abundance of natural resources and inexhaustible human enthusiasm, and by our relative isolation from the malignant problems of older civilizations. The world is indeed one global village. We live among determined, well-educated, and strongly motivated competitors. We compete with them for international standing and markets, not only with products but also with the ideas of our laboratories and neighborhood workshops. America's position in the world may once have been reasonably secure with only a few exceptionally well-trained men and women. It is no longer.

The risk is not only that the Japanese make automobiles more efficiently than Americans and have government subsidies for development and export. It is not just that the South Koreans recently built the world's most efficient steel mill, or that American machine tools, once the pride of the world, are being displaced by German products. It is also that these developments signify a redistribution of trained capability throughout the globe. Knowledge, learning, information, and skilled intelligence are the new raw materials of international commerce and are today spreading throughout the world as vigorously as miracle drugs, synthetic fertilizers, and blue jeans did earlier. If only to keep and improve on the slim competitive edge we still retain in world markets, we must dedicate ourselves to the reform of our educational system for the benefit of all—old and young alike, affluent and poor, majority and minority. Learning is the indispensable investment required for success in the "information age" we are entering.

Our concern, however, goes well beyond matters such as industry and commerce. It also includes the intellectual, moral, and spiritual strengths of our people which knit together the very fabric of our society. The people of the United States need to know that individuals in our society who do not possess the levels of skill, literacy, and training essential to this new era will be effectively disenfranchised, not simply from the material rewards that accompany competent performance, but also from the chance to participate fully in our national life. A high level of shared education is essential to a free, democratic society and to the fostering of a common culture, especially in a country that prides itself on pluralism and individual freedom.

For our country to function, citizens must be able to reach some common understandings on complex issues, often on short notice and on the basis of conflicting or incomplete evidence. Education helps form these common understandings, a point Thomas Jefferson made long ago in his justly famous dictum:

> I know no safe depository of the ultimate powers of the society but the people themselves; and if we think them not enlightened enough to exercise their control with a wholesome discretion, the remedy is not to take it from them but to inform their discretion.

Part of what is at risk is the promise first made on this continent: All, regardless of race or class or economic status, are entitled to a fair chance and to the tools for developing their individual powers of mind and spirit to the utmost. This promise means that all children by virtue of their own efforts, competently guided, can hope to attain the mature and informed judgment needed to secure gainful employment, and to manage their own lives, thereby serving not only their own interests but also the progress of society itself.

Indicators of the Risk

The educational dimensions of the risk before us have been amply documented in testimony received by the Commission. For example:

○ International comparisons of student achievement, completed a decade ago, reveal that on 19 academic tests American students were never first or second and, in comparison with other industrialized nations, were last seven times.

○ Some 23 million American adults are functionally illiterate by the simplest tests of everyday reading, writing, and comprehension.

○ About 13 percent of all 17-year-olds in the United States can be considered functionally illiterate. Functional illiteracy among minority youth may run as high as 40 percent.

○ Average achievement of high school students on most standardized tests is now lower than 26 years ago when Sputnik was launched.

○ Over half the population of gifted students do not match their tested ability with comparable achievement in school.

- The College Board's Scholastic Aptitude Tests (SAT) demonstrate a virtually unbroken decline from 1963 to 1980. Average verbal scores fell over 50 points and average mathematics scores dropped nearly 40 points (see Exhibit 1).

- College Board achievement tests also reveal consistent declines in recent years in such subjects as physics and English.

- Both the number and proportion of students demonstrating superior achievement on the SATs (i.e., those with scores of 650 or higher) have also dramatically declined.

- Many 17-year-olds do not possess the "higher order" intellectual skills we should expect of them. Nearly 40 percent cannot draw inferences from written material; only one-fifth can write a persuasive essay; and only one-third can solve a mathematics problem requiring several steps.

- There was a steady decline in science achievement scores of U.S. 17-year-olds as measured by national assessments of science in 1969, 1973, and 1977.

- Between 1975 and 1980, remedial mathematics courses in public 4-year colleges increased by 72 percent and now constitute one-quarter of all mathematics courses taught in those institutions.

- Average tested achievement of students graduating from college is also lower.

- Business and military leaders complain that they are required to spend millions of dollars on costly remedial education and training programs in such basic skills as reading, writing, spelling, and computation. The Department of the Navy, for example, reported to the Commission that one-quarter of its recent recruits

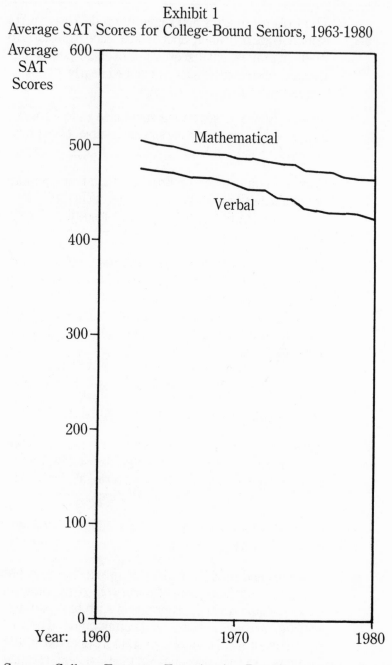

Exhibit 1
Average SAT Scores for College-Bound Seniors, 1963-1980

Average SAT Scores

Mathematical

Verbal

Year: 1960   1970   1980

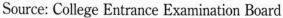

Source: College Entrance Examination Board

10

cannot read at the ninth grade level, the minimum needed simply to understand written safety instructions. Without remedial work they cannot even begin, much less complete, the sophisticated training essential in much of the modern military.

These deficiencies come at a time when the demand for highly skilled workers in new fields is accelerating rapidly (see Exhibit 2): For example:

○ Computers and computer-controlled equipment are penetrating every aspect of our lives—homes, factories, and offices.

○ One estimate indicates that by the turn of the century millions of jobs will involve laser technology and robotics.

○ Technology is radically transforming a host of other occupations. They include health care, medical science, energy production, food processing, construction, and the building, repair, and maintenance of sophisticated scientific, educational, military, and industrial equipment.

Analysts examining these indicators of student performance and the demands for new skills have made some chilling observations. Educational researcher Paul Hurd concluded at the end of a thorough national survey of student achievement that within the context of the modern scientific revolution, "We are raising a new generation of Americans that is scientifically and technologically illiterate." In a similar vein, John Slaughter, a former Director of the National Science Foundation, warned of "a growing chasm between a small scientific and technological elite and a citizenry ill-informed, indeed uninformed, on issues with a science component."

But the problem does not stop there, nor do all observers see it the same way. Some worry that schools may

Exhibit 2

Occupations With Projected Highest Percentage Growth in Job Openings, 1980-1990

Occupation	Estimated % Change In Jobs, 1980-1990
Computer Service Technicians	93-112
Computer Systems Analysts	68-80
Business Machine Operators	60-74
Dental Hygienists	67
Computer Programmers	49-60
Physical Therapists	51-59
Health Service Administrators	43-53
Aerospace Engineers	43-52
Registered Nurses	40-47
Electrical Engineers	35-47

Source: U.S. Labor Department, Bureau of Labor Statistics

emphasize such rudiments as reading and computation at the expense of other essential skills such as comprehension, analysis, solving problems, and drawing conclusions. Still others are concerned that an over-emphasis on technical and occupational skills will leave little time for studying the arts and humanities that so enrich daily life, help maintain civility, and develop a sense of community. Knowledge of the humanities, they maintain, must be harnessed to science and technology if the latter are to remain creative and humane, just as the humanities need to be informed by science and technology if they are to remain relevant to the human condition. Another analyst, Paul Copperman, has drawn a sobering conclusion. Until now (see Exhibit 3), he has noted:

> Each generation of Americans has outstripped its parents in education, in literacy, and in economic attainment. For the first time in the history of our country, the educational skills of one generation will not surpass, will not equal, will not even approach, those of their parents.

It is important, of course, to recognize that *the average citizen* today is better educated and more knowledgeable than the average citizen of a generation ago—more literate, and exposed to more mathematics, literature, and science. The positive impact of this fact on the well-being of our country and the lives of our people cannot be overstated. Nevertheless, *the average graduate* of our schools and colleges today is not as well-educated as the average graduate of 25 or 35 years ago, when a much smaller proportion of our population completed high school and college. The negative impact of this fact likewise cannot be overstated.

Exhibit 3
Level of School Completed by Persons Age 25 and Over,
1920-1980

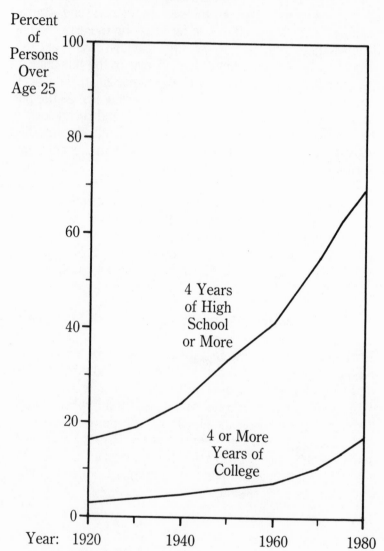

Percent of Persons Over Age 25

4 Years of High School or More

4 or More Years of College

Year: 1920 1940 1960 1980

Source: U.S. Department of Commerce, Bureau of Census

Hope and Frustration

Statistics and their interpretation by experts show only the surface dimension of the difficulties we face. Beneath them lies a tension between hope and frustration that characterizes current attitudes about education at every level.

We have heard the voices of high school and college students, school board members, and teachers; of leaders of industry, minority groups, and higher education; of parents and State officials. We could hear the hope evident in their commitment to quality education and in their descriptions of outstanding programs and schools. We could also hear the intensity of their frustration, a growing impatience with shoddiness in many walks of American life, and the complaint that this shoddiness is too often reflected in our schools and colleges. Their frustration threatens to overwhelm their hope.

What lies behind this emerging national sense of frustration can be described as both a dimming of personal expectations and the fear of losing a shared vision for America.

On the personal level the student, the parent, and the caring teacher all perceive that a basic promise is not being kept. More and more young people emerge from high school ready neither for college nor for work. This predicament becomes more acute as the knowledge base continues its rapid expansion, the number of traditional jobs shrinks, and new jobs demand greater sophistication and preparation.

On a broader scale, we sense that this undertone of frustration has significant political implications, for it cuts across ages, generations, races, and political and economic groups. We have come to understand that the public will demand that educational and political leaders act forcefully and effectively on these issues. Indeed, such demands have already appeared and could well become a unifying national preoccupation. This unity, however, can be achieved only if we avoid the unproductive tendency of some to search for scapegoats among the victims, such as the beleaguered teachers.

On the positive side is the significant movement by political and educational leaders to search for solutions—so far centering largely on the nearly desperate need for increased support for the teaching of mathematics and science. This movement is but a start on what we believe is a larger and more educationally encompassing need to improve teaching and learning in fields such as English, history, geography, economics, and foreign languages. We believe this movement must be broadened and directed toward reform and excellence throughout education.

Excellence in Education

We define "excellence" to mean several related things. At the level of the *individual learner,* it means performing on the boundary of individual ability in ways that test and push back personal limits, in school and in the workplace. Excellence characterizes a *school or college* that sets high expectations and goals for all learners, then tries in every way possible to help students reach them. Excellence characterizes a *society* that has adopted these policies, for it will then be prepared through the education and skill of its people to respond to the challenges of a rapidly changing world. Our Nation's people and its schools and colleges must be committed to achieving excellence in all these senses.

We do not believe that a public commitment to excellence and educational reform must be made at the expense of a strong public commitment to the equitable treatment of our diverse population. The twin goals of equity and high-quality schooling have profound and practical meaning for our economy and society, and we cannot permit one to yield to the other either in principle or in practice. To do so would deny young people their chance to learn and live according to their aspirations and abilities. It also would lead to a generalized accommodation to mediocrity in our society on the one hand or the creation of an undemocratic elitism on the other.

Our goal must be to develop the talents of all to their fullest. Attaining that goal requires that we expect and assist all students to work to the limits of their capabilities. We should expect schools to have genuinely high standards rather than minimum ones, and parents to support and encourage their children to make the most of their talents and abilities.

The search for solutions to our educational problems must also include a commitment to life-long learning. The task of rebuilding our system of learning is enormous and must be properly understood and taken seriously: Although a million and a half new workers enter the economy each year from our schools and colleges, the adults working today will still make up about 75 percent of the workforce in the year 2000. These workers, and new entrants into the workforce, will need further education and retraining if they—and we as a Nation— are to thrive and prosper.

The Learning Society

In a world of ever-accelerating competition and change in the conditions of the workplace, of ever-greater danger, and of ever-larger opportunities for those prepared to meet them, educational reform should focus on the goal of creating a Learning Society. At the heart of such a society is the commitment to a set of values and to a system of education that affords all members the opportunity to stretch their minds to full capacity, from early childhood through adulthood, learning more as the world itself changes. Such a society has as a basic foundation the idea that education is important not only because of what it contributes to one's career goals but also because of the value it adds to the general quality of one's life. Also at the heart of the Learning Society are educational opportunities extending far beyond the traditional institutions of learning, our schools and colleges. They extend into homes and workplaces; into libraries, art galleries, museums, and science centers; indeed, into every place where the individual can develop and mature in work and life. In our view, formal schooling in youth is the essential foundation for learning throughout one's life. But without life-long learning, one's skills will become rapidly dated.

In contrast to the ideal of the Learning Society, however, we find that for too many people education means doing the minimum work necessary for the moment, then coasting through life on what may have been learned in its first quarter. But this should not surprise us because we tend to express our educational standards and expectations largely in terms of "minimum requirements." And where there should be a coherent continuum of learning, we have none, but instead an often incoherent, outdated patchwork quilt. Many individual, sometimes heroic, examples of schools and colleges of great merit do exist. Our findings and testimony confirm the vitality of a number of notable schools and programs, but their very distinction stands out against a vast mass shaped by tensions and pressures that inhibit systematic academic and vocational achievement for the majority of students. In some metropolitan areas basic literacy has become the goal rather than the starting point. In some colleges maintaining enrollments is of greater day-to-day concern than maintaining rigorous academic standards. And the ideal of academic excellence as the primary goal of schooling seems to be fading across the board in American education.

Thus, we issue this call to all who care about America and its future: to parents and students; to teachers, administrators, and school board members; to colleges and industry; to union members and military leaders; to governors and State legislators; to the President; to members of Congress and other public officials; to members of learned and scientific societies; to the print and electronic media; to concerned citizens everywhere. America is at risk.

We are confident that America can address this risk. If the tasks we set forth are initiated now and our recommendations are fully realized over the next several years, we can expect reform of our Nation's schools, colleges, and universities. This would also reverse the current declining trend—a trend that stems more from weakness of purpose, confusion of vision, underuse of talent, and lack of leadership, than from conditions beyond our control.

The Tools at Hand

It is our conviction that the essential raw materials needed to reform our educational system are waiting to be mobilized through effective leadership:

○ the natural abilities of the young that cry out to be developed and the undiminished concern of parents for the well-being of their children;

○ the commitment of the Nation to high retention rates in schools and colleges and to full access to education for all;

○ the persistent and authentic American dream that superior performance can raise one's state in life and shape one's own future;

○ the dedication, against all odds, that keeps teachers serving in schools and colleges, even as the rewards diminish;

○ our better understanding of learning and teaching and the implications of this knowledge for school practice, and the numerous examples of local success as a result of superior effort and effective dissemination;

○ the ingenuity of our policymakers, scientists, State and local educators, and scholars in formulating solutions once problems are better understood;

○ the traditional belief that paying for education is an investment in ever-renewable human resources that are more durable and flexible than capital plant and equipment, and the availability in this country of sufficient financial means to invest in education;

○ the equally sound tradition, from the Northwest Ordinance of 1787 until today, that the Federal Government should supplement State, local, and other resources to foster key national educational goals; and

○ the voluntary efforts of individuals, businesses, and parent and civic groups to cooperate in strengthening educational programs.

These raw materials, combined with the unparalleled array of educational organizations in America, offer us the possibility to create a Learning Society, in which public, private, and parochial schools; colleges and universities; vocational and technical schools and institutes; libraries; science centers, museums, and other cultural institutions; and corporate training and retraining programs offer opportunities and choices for all to learn throughout life.

The Public's Commitment

Of all the tools at hand, the public's support for education is the most powerful. In a message to a National Academy of Sciences meeting in May 1982, President Reagan commented on this fact when he said:

> This public awareness—and I hope public action—is long overdue. . . . This country was built on American respect for education. . . . Our challenge now is to create a resurgence of that thirst for education that typifies our Nation's history.

The most recent (1982) Gallup Poll of the *Public's Attitudes Toward the Public Schools* strongly supported a theme heard during our hearings: People are steadfast in their belief that education is the major foundation for the future strength of this country. They even considered education more important than developing the best industrial system or the strongest military force, perhaps because they understood education as the cornerstone of both. They also held that education is "extremely important" to one's future success, and that public education should be the top priority for additional Federal funds. Education occupied first place among 12 funding categories considered in the survey—above health care, welfare, and military defense, with 55 percent selecting public education as one of their first three choices. Very clearly, the public understands the primary importance of education as the foundation for a satisfying life, an enlightened and civil society, a strong economy, and a secure Nation.

At the same time, the public has no patience with undemanding and superfluous high school offerings. In another survey, more than 75 percent of all those questioned believed every student planning to go to college should take 4 years of mathematics, English, history/U.S. government, and science, with more than 50 percent adding 2 years each of a foreign language and economics or business. The public even supports requiring much of this curriculum for students who do not plan to go to college. These standards far exceed the strictest high school graduation requirements of any State today, and they also exceed the admission standards of all but a handful of our most selective colleges and universities.

Another dimension of the public's support offers the prospect of constructive reform. The best term to characterize it may simply be the honorable word "patriotism." Citizens know intuitively what some of the best economists have shown in their research, that education is one of the chief engines of a society's material well-being. They know, too, that education is the common bond of a pluralistic society and helps tie us to other cultures around the globe. Citizens also know in their bones that the safety of the United States depends principally on the wit, skill, and spirit of a self-confident people, today and tomorrow. It is, therefore, essential—especially in a period of long-term decline in educational achievement—for government at all levels to affirm its responsibility for nurturing the Nation's intellectual capital.

And perhaps most important, citizens know and believe that the meaning of America to the rest of the world must be something better than it seems to many today. Americans like to think of this Nation as the preeminent country for generating the great ideas and material benefits for all mankind. The citizen is dismayed at a steady 15-year decline in industrial productivity, as one great American industry after another falls to world competition. The citizen wants the country to act on the belief, expressed in our hearings and by the large majority in the Gallup Poll, that education should be at the top of the Nation's agenda.

Chapter 3
Commissioned Research

Findings of the study were shaped significantly by research papers executed by selected USA and international experts. Summaries of their analysis, findings, and recommendations follow. Order of summaries is according to the author's last name.

Clifford Adelman 　　**National Institute** 　　**of Education** 　　**Washington, D.C.**	**"A Study of High** **School Transcripts,** **1964-1981"**	**81 pages**

This paper reanalyzed existing transcript data from: (1) the Study of Academic Prediction and Growth (High School Class of 1969); and (2) the New Youth Cohort of the National Longitudinal Study of Labor Market Experience (High School Classes of 1975-1981) in terms of various measures of the quantity of schooling, and in relation to changes in college graduation requirements between 1967 and 1974. Major findings discussed in this paper include: (1) The average credit value of academic courses in high schools has declined considerably since the late 1960s, indicating that less time is being allocated for them and that students are spending less time in the academic curriculum; (2) High school students on all tracks are spending more time in and receiving more credit for "personal service and development" courses, a trend which accounts largely for the results in (1); (3) The dominant student track in high school is now the "General Track" — curriculum dominated by survey, remedial, and personal service courses — and many students in this track go on to college; (4) The secondary school curriculum has become diffused and fragmented over the past 15 years, as have college courses and degrees; and (5) Grade inflation, while significant has not been as pervasive as assumed, and its locations and sources in the curriculum do not fit easy assumptions.

Joseph Adelson The University of Michigan, Ann Arbor	"Twenty-Five Years of American Education: An Interpretation"	41 pages

This paper explores the ideological changes which have influenced American education during the past 25 years. Gradual shifting of values and fluctuating attitudes are examined in the broad areas of authority, educational theory, the idea of merit, and moral perspectives. It is pointed out that public dissatisfaction with the schools has been felt for well over a decade and that it has been responsive to the actual vicissitudes of American schooling, specifically the easing of both academic and disciplinary demands. It is also noted that the public's attitude toward schooling is not shared by a great many experts in education, who may agree that there has been a decline in quality, but see this as the price to be paid for universal education. In probing changes in the philosophy of education, an effort is made to clarify the reasons for the loss of consensus as to the functions of the schools and the values they are meant to embody and teach.

Catherine P. Ailes Francis W. Rushing SRI International, Arlington, Virginia	"A Summary Report on the Educational Systems of the United States and the Soviet Union: Comparative Analysis"	40 pages

Education in the U.S.S.R. is much more strongly oriented toward the scientific and technical fields than is that of the United States. This may be an asset in the development of specialists with the ability to attain the short-term technological targets of the Soviet economic plan. However, the more flexible, theoretical, broader-based higher education system in the United States may produce specialists with an ability to innovate, with an ability to adapt to technological change, and with a greater latitude for interfield mobility as the demands of the economy change. A comparative analysis is presented of: (1) the structure of education in the two countries; (2) general education — elementary and secondary; (3) transition from incomplete to complete secondary education; (4) specialized secondary schools; (5) higher education; and (6) graduate training. A set of statistical tables providing a quantitative comparison of entrance, enrollment, and completion of the various stages in the educational process in the two countries is appended.

Alexander W. Astin University of California, Los Angeles	"Excellence and Equity in American Education"	30 pages

The "value-added" conception of excellence in education, unlike any traditional view, focuses on the ability of a school or college to affect its students favorably and equitably. It focuses on changes in the student from the beginning to the end of the educational program. The "value-added" approach would involve the testing of students entering a school or college for the first time to determine their entering levels of competence for purposes of counseling and course placement. These initial "pretest" scores would not only provide both students and teachers with information about the student's specific strengths and weaknesses, but they would also constitute a baseline against which to measure later student progress ("value-added"). Following the completion of appropriate courses or programs of study, the same or similar tests would be readministered to measure student growth. This approach, unlike traditional measures such as the reputational view, the resources view, or the outcomes view, promotes equity because it diverts attention away from mere acquisition of resources and focuses instead on their effective utilization. Any school is capable of attaining a significant degree of "excellence" through this method.

Alexander W. Astin University of California, Los Angeles	"The American Freshman, 1966-1981: Some Implications for Educational Policy and Practice"	59 pages

Trends in the characteristics of students who go directly on to college after completing high school have been surveyed for the past 16 years. Findings on significant trends are cited and analyzed: (1) Students are less well prepared academically than entering students of 10 or 15 years ago. (2) Declining academic skill levels are reflected in the declining rate of college attendance among high school graduates (especially white males) and the sharp decline in student majors in mathematics and fields that require verbal skills. (3) Declining academic skills have been accompanied by declines in other areas of student competency and declining interest among male students in pursuing graduate study. (4) Today's students are more interested in business, engineering, and computer science, and less interested in education, social science, fine and performing arts, and the humanities. (5) Today's students are more materialistic, more interested in power and status, less altruistic, and less inclined to be concerned about social issues and problems. (6) Freshmen of today are substantially less liberal in their political identification than freshmen of 10 years ago. (7) Compared to earlier generations, today's female college students are more likely to be pursuing careers in business, medicine, law, and engineering, and significantly less likely to pursue careers in teaching and nursing. (8) There have been substantial increases in representation of women and disadvantaged minorities among entering freshmen.

Herman Blake University of California, Santa Cruz	"Demographic Change and Curriculum: New Students in Higher Education"	42 pages

Oakes College at the University of California Santa Cruz (UCSC) is a residential liberal arts college for individuals from minority groups, "new students" who are from poverty backgrounds or are the first in their families to go to college, and women re-entering school. These students are more likely to need remedial or tutorial help than their counterparts in other UCSC colleges. Curriculum focuses on the experience of ethnic minorities in the United States, and on science. Oakes College offers first-year basic skills courses in writing, mathematics, computer literacy, and study skills; these courses serve as links for students between their pre-collegiate experience and self-identification in their new university experience. The intensive lower-division science program is geared to the needs of "new students"; courses in biology, chemistry, and mathematics are designed to feed students into campus-wide majors at appropriate points. Since faculty members, many of whom are women and/or members of minority groups, serve as teachers, role models, and student counselors (with possible detriment to academic research work and professional development), a support program provides released time for individual endeavors. Tables on the changing demographic profile in California are appended, illustrating the educational needs which gave rise to the founding of Oakes College.

Richard I. Brod
   The Modern Language
   Association
   New York, New York
Nicholas Farnham
   The International
   Council on the Future
   of the University
   New York, New York
William V. Mayer
   Biological Sciences
   Curriculum Study
   Boulder, Colorado
Robert A. McCaughey
   Barnard College,
   New York, New York
	"University Entrance
	Examinations and
	Performance
	Expectations"
		57 pages

Consisting of four papers, this study examines university entrance examinations in France, Great Britain, and West Germany and compares them to similar tests in the United States on the basis of three subjects: world history, language study, and biology. The first paper, "The Relationship of the Examinations to the Secondary School Age Group" (Nicholas

Farnham), discusses the following examinations: (1) the French Baccalaureate; (2) the German Arbitur; (3) the British GCE-A Level (the advanced level of the General Certificate Examination); (4) the International Baccalaureate (accepted by universities in all countries); and (5) the United States Advanced Placement Test (APT) and Achievement Tests. The second paper, "World History" (Robert A. McCaughey), discusses separately the breadth of each examination and evaluates the capacity of each for self criticism (of its own country's history). The author finds no reason to believe that American students taking the APT are less equipped for serious study than are European students. The third paper, "Language Study," by Richard I. Brod, looks at each country's tests for second language competency. The author finds the United States' College Entrance Examination Board test lacking because it does not approach the universality of the other countries' tests. The author finds the APT much more satisfactory. The fourth paper, "Biology" (William V. Mayer), after discussing each country's test in detail, finds the United States' Achievement Tests have breadth in the subject matter of the test questions but no depth. Although the author feels the APT is better, in comparison, the United States biology examinations do not compare well. They are less demanding, more detail laden, require no writing, and do not concentrate on higher educational objectives.

Barbara B. Burn	**"An Analytic**	**82 pages**
Christopher H. Hurn	**Comparison of**	
University of	**Educational Systems"**	
Massachusetts,		
Amherst		

This comparative evaluation of the differing educational systems in North America, Europe, the USSR, and Japan examines the goals and values of these systems. It is pointed out that Americans value equality, practicality, and utility and that they are both individualistic and suspicious of government authority. Contrasts between these values and those implicit in the societies in Western Europe, Russia, and Japan are explored. The structure and organization of educational systems is also discussed. Judgments are offered concerning the effective locus of power in such matters as school organization, curriculum, and personnel policies. The Soviet Union, France, and Japan are identified as highly centralized systems and comparison is made between the structure of these systems and those of Western Europe (mixed local, regional, and central control), and America and Canada, where local control is usually decisive. The selectivity of these systems is discussed as they reflect cultural attitudes toward the upward mobility of citizens. Differences and similarities in educational outcomes and policy implications between the systems are also pointed out, and special consideration is given to changes in attitudes toward schooling over the past few decades. Appendix I contains an analysis of science and mathematics education in the Soviet Union and Japan. Appendix II discusses equivalencies in secondary schooling in the United States, Canada, Japan, the Soviet Union, Japan, and West Germany. Statistics on school enrollments are presented in tabular format.

Philip Cusick **Michigan State** **University,** **East Lansing**	**"Secondary Public** **Schools in America"**	**34 pages**

Comprehensiveness, local control, and public funding combine to create public secondary schools that serve the educational needs of all students and are open to influence from people outside the school structure. From these sectors come demands for accountability; community influence; and a heavy commitment of resources to maintaining good attendance, discipline, and public relations, which are the responsibility of the school administration. Secondary school curriculum consists of a broad range of diverse courses. This diversity is the result of perceived student needs and, in particular, the public schools' vulnerability to pressure from advocacy groups who, by their special demands, shape and increase curriculum offerings. Responsibility for curriculum falls to the teachers, who must instruct and relate to students, and not burden the administration with disciplinary problems. Fragmented, diverse, open, and fluid curriculum responds to the needs and demands of students with widely divergent abilities, attitudes toward education, and career plans. The critical factor which differentiates a "good" school from one not so good is the orientation of the majority of the students in the school toward superior academic education.

Walter Doyle   **"Academic Work"**   **87 pages**
    University of Texas
        at Austin

This paper is focused on a relatively new emphasis in education research: the nature of academic work contained in the curriculum of elementary and secondary schools, how that work is organized and accomplished in classrooms, and what modifications in academic work are likely to increase student achievement. The paper is divided into two major sections. The first section is devoted to an analysis of the intellectual demands inherent in different forms of academic work. Of special importance in this section is the recent work on cognitive processes which underlie school tasks. The second section is directed to studies of how academic work is carried on in classroom environments. Particular attention in this section is given to the ways in which social and evaluative conditions in classrooms affect students' reactions to work. Each section contains an analysis of implications for improving the quality of academic work in classrooms and thus increasing student achievement. Also present is an extensive bibliography (21 pages).

Kenneth Duckworth   **"Some Ideas About**   **20 pages**
    University of   **Student Cognition,**
    Oregon, Eugene   **Motivation and Work"**

A critique is offered of three papers on the student's role in learning. The first, by Robert Sternberg and Richard Wagner, makes connections between cognitive processing of information and the metacognitive processing of one's own approach to a situation and the information contained therein. The second, by Deborah Stipek, implies that metacognitive processing depends upon intrinsic motivation and may be stunted by structured extrinsic reinforcement. The third, by Walter Doyle, holds that evaluation and control pressures in classrooms are detrimental to intelligence and motivation to learn. Each paper is synthesized and a set of recommendations is offered for the redefinition of the student role in learning. Four approaches are discussed: (1) build on the foundations of direct instruction; (2) distinguish short-term and long-term values of learning; (3) develop student capacity for self-management of work; and (4) ground higher-order learning on ideals and exemplars. A discussion is presented of the work conditions required for teachers to implement the sort of curricular ideas suggested in the papers, focusing on management of teachers' agendas, resources, and incentives. Implications for school administrators and policy makers are considered.

Max A. Eckstein
  Queens College/
  City of New York
  Flushing
Susanne Shafer
  Arizona State
  University, Tempe
Kenneth Travers
  University of Illinois,
  Champaign-Urbana
	"A Comparative
	Review of Curriculum:
	Mathematics and
	International Studies
	in the Secondary
	Schools of Five
	Countries"
		115 pages

This paper describes curriculum content in two areas — mathematics and international studies — in the secondary schools of Canada, Japan, West Germany, the USSR, and the United States. Relevant background on teacher preparation and on the structure and organization of secondary schooling in each country is introduced to provide a context for the information provided. After the introduction, the paper's second part summarizes major conceptual and methodological issues in comparative studies and in comparative curriculum. In the third section, the content of the mathematics programs is presented with data on when that content is introduced into the program in each country. A sampling of instructional practices from various countries which may have relevance to mathematics education in the United States is included, and issues in mathematics education are examined. The international studies component of the broader social studies curriculum is described and discussed in the fourth section, and case histories of the curriculum in each country are presented. In the fifth part, concluding observations draw attention to the issues of the nature, possibilities, and problems of comparative curriculum study, the two curriculum areas, teachers and instruction, and considerations of curriculum change and policy making.

Eleanor Farrar
  The Huron Institute
  Cambridge,
  Massachusetts
Matthew B. Miles
  Center for Policy
  Research
  New York, New York
Barbara Neufeld
  The Huron Institute
  Cambridge,
  Massachusetts

"A Review of Effective   40 pages
Schools Research:
Implications for
Practice and Research"

The effective schools movement, a program which involves school staff in diagnosis of problems, decisions on correcting them, research on the effectiveness of various alternatives, and training and assistance with imrpovement efforts, has focused, up until now, on elementary schools. The feasibility of transferring these programs to high schools is examined. It is pointed out that, since the research base for the programs derives from studies of minority urban elementary schools, the school characteristics identified are not typical of the average high school; also, because the research base emphasizes achievement at the elementary level, many other goals that are typical of high schools are not addressed. A discussion of the differences between high schools and elementary schools considers: (1) diversity of high school academic and social objectives; (2) large size of high schools; (3) organizational complexity; (4) subject-oriented faculty; (5) frequent movement of students from class to class; (6) tracking of students; (7) complex administrative role of the principal; (8) faculty resistance; (9) student goals and attitudes toward school; and (10) parent and community attitudes toward school responsibilities.

Zelda Gamson	"A Little Light on the	74 pages
University of	Subject: Keeping	
Michigan, Ann Arbor	General and Liberal	
	Education Alive"	

This paper on the state of general and liberal education in the United States discusses a project which sought to examine and improve general and liberal education program at the higher education level. The first part of this paper delineates the undermining of liberal education in the nation's colleges and universities following World War II. The second part describes National Project IV, which brought together representatives from 14 diverse colleges and universities to examine conceptions and practices of liberal education from the perspective of their own programs. The third section presents a discussion on the context and content of the 14 programs as they operate within the organizational structure of their particular educational community. Comments and reflections from students in the 14 programs are presented in the fourth part. The fifth part contains a summary of the individual and social benefits accruing from these general and liberal education programs and offers recommendations for improvement. Appendix A summarizes major features of the institutions and the programs that were part of National Project IV, and their curriculum designs. The second and third appendixes summarize characteristics of the 14 institutions, and characteristics of students participating in the programs.

William E. Gardner	"Certification and	52 pages
University of	Accreditation: Back-	
Minnesota,	ground, Issue Analysis,	
Minneapolis	and Recommendations"	
John R. Palmer		
University of		
Wisconsin, Madison		

An analysis of issues concerning the certification of teachers and the accreditation and approval of teacher education institutions is presented. In the first part, generally accepted definitions of certification, licensure, program review, and accreditation are clarified. A brief historical overview is presented of the state's role in controlling licensure, and the growth of the National Education Association (NEA) and the National Council for Accreditation of Teacher Education (NCATE) is described. Key issues regarding certification and accreditation guide the discussion of major strategies for imrpovement in the second part: (1) certification based on approved programs or qualifying examinations; (2) specific rules governing college programs and general certification; (3) renewal of teaching licenses; (4) incompetent teachers or low-quality programs; (5) rule-making process; (6) attraction of more academically able students; (7) social needs to recruit people from protected groups; (8) five year or longer teacher education programs; (9) teacher supply and demand; and (10) duplicate and redundant program review standards or procedures. The paper's third part offers recommendations and conclusions concerning general teacher education standards, identification of teacher competence, examination of entry-level teachers, teacher internships, certificate renewal, redundancy of NCATE and state agency program-approval, restructuring of NCATE process, and elimination of substandard teacher education programs.

| Thomas L. Good University of Missouri — Columbia | "What Is Learned in Schools: Responding to School Demands, Grades K-6" | 88 pages |

Individual teacher behaviors, characteristics, and instructional methods make an important difference in what and how well students learn. Children enter school with a wide variety of differences in family background and aspirations, expectations, and previous learning. Research on learning in the home, nursery school, and kindergarten points out the differences between the learning environments of school and home settings, and differences between teachers' and parents' expectations and approaches to teaching. Once in the school environment, the student encounters a variety of instructional styles and classroom expectations in teachers which often pose problems as they move from class to class or grade to grade. In addition, a student's background may conflict with the general school culture or that of a particular teacher. In this paper, which discusses current trends and research on this topic, questions are raised about instructional practices such as tracking, pull-out instruction, and ability grouping on the grounds that they often create difficult teaching/learning situations. The general effects of teacher expectations on student performance are discussed with suggestions for improvements.

Thomas L. Good
Gail M. Hinkel
    University of
Missouri — Columbia
"Schooling in America: 101 pages
Some Descriptive and
Explanatory
Statements"

This paper briefly characterizes schooling in America in broad terms, describes what is known about the relationship between teacher behavior and student behavior, and explains why certain classroom characteristics are related to student achievement. The paper begins with a description, of classroom practices in American schools, based in part upon selected papers that have been presented to the National Commission on Excellence in Education. Findings cited in this paper indicate that teachers vary widely in: (1) use of classroom time; (2) management of classroom activities; (3) selection and design of classroom learning tasks; (4) teaching and communicating with students; and (5) expectations and academic standards held for themselves, peers, classes, and individual students. It is noted that research also demonstrates that these aspects of classroom life are related to student achievement. This paper describes these research findings, particularly in the areas of: (1) time and learning; (2) classroom management; (3) active teaching; (4) curriculum content and academic work structures; (5) teacher expectations; (6) student influence; and (7) motivation and personal investment. Research findings are used to suggest how particular patterns of classroom behavior hinder or facilitate student achievement. References are included.

Donald B. Holsinger State University of New York, Albany	"Time, Content and Expectations as Predictors of School Achievement in the U.S.A. and Other Developed Countries: A Review of IEA Evidence"	58 pages

An overview is presented of the scope and findings of the International Association for the Evaluation of Educational Achievement (IEA) studies, which analyzed student achievement in 22 nations, one of which was the United States. Using these findings, this paper identifies national differences in the performance of pupils representing the United States and other nations which are part of a set of relatively more developed countries. Three principal considerations in the differences found — time spent on the subject, curriculum content, and student, teacher, and family expectations — are discussed, along with the principal findings: (1) Among more advanced countries and students, there were no marked deviations in the pattern of achievement test scores; (2) Time given to instruction and opportunity to learn were two key characteristics associated with high test scores and achievement; (3) Curriculum content was consistently and significantly related to achievement scores in the less developed countries and to only a slightly smaller degree in the more developed countries; and (4) Inferences with respect to the place of expectations in student achievement were largely limited to personal expectations and motivation of the individual student.

Kenneth R. Howey University of Minnesota, Minneapolis	"Charting Directions for Preservice Teacher Education"	51 pages

This paper on the future of preservice teacher education examines the question of whether a crisis exists today in schools and in teacher education. It is noted that judgments vary, given different perspectives and vantage points for observation, and that a reliable assessment of the current health of schooling and teacher education is difficult. Possible future directions for teacher education are suggested, and discernable conditions and events on the horizon are examined. A major conclusion is that the only way heightened or extended expectations can reasonably be accommodated are through more formalized and shared responsibilities by schools with other socially responsible parties. No major reform is envisioned in initial teacher education. Emphasis in this paper is placed on a multi-faceted approach to incremental improvements in the quality of teachers and teaching. Strategies for improving the quality of teaching are identified: (1) improve methods and procedures for recruiting and selecting teachers; (2) upgrade the quality of and/or extend, programs for preparing teachers; (3) improve evaluation of teachers and teacher education programs; and (4) critically reexamine teachers' role expectations and school conditions.

| Paul DeHart Hurd
  Stanford University,
  California | "An Overview of
Science Education in
the United States and
Selected Foreign
Countries" | 128 pages |

This report, on science education in the United States, East Germany, West Germany, China, Japan, and the USSR, has 12 chapters. Chapter 1 presents an overview of precollege science education in the United States from 1940 to 1970. In chapter 2, the status of science education from 1970 to 1980 focuses on elementary and secondary school science instruction, traditional science curriculum, science instruction in all the countries, and science enrollments and school requirements. Chapter 3 presents information on science facilities. Chapter 4 summarizes findings about science teachers, problems of science teacher supply and demand, and inservice education and professional development for science teachers. In chapter 5, a comparison is made between nonschool science education in the United States and the selected foreign countries, and similar comparison is presented in the 6th chapter on instructional practices in science teaching. Science achievement and students' attitudes toward science are compared in the 7th chapter. The discussion in chapter 8 deals with differences and similarities of parental attitudes toward science education in the United States and other countries. A global view of research and development in science education is offered in the 9th chapter. In the 10th and 11th chapters, problems, issues, and concerns in science education in the United States and actions being taken are examined. The final chapter offers a synoptic overview of science education in foreign countries.

Torsten Husen University of Stockholm, Sweden	"A Cross-National Perspective on Assessing the Quality of Learning"	56 pages

A ten-year research effort, conducted by the International Association for the Evaluation of Educational Achievement (IEA), explored the relative merits and failings of different national systems of education in the United States and in Western and Eastern Europe. The first section of this report deals with trends in American education as seen through European eyes. The American system is viewed as a vehicle for upward social mobility and as a means of solving or ameliorating social problems. In the second section, the theoretical framework and research strategy of the IEA are described, as well as the difficulties encountered in comparing systems of education that are widely different in function and philosophy. The way individual differences are perceived and taken into account in organizing formal education in various national systems is considered in the third section. Comparisons are made of the American model of comprehensive education for all students, the Western European model, with early transfer of selected elite students to academic secondary schools, and the Soviet unitary school that integrates all types of schools. The fourth section elaborates on comparisons between comprehensive and selective systems of education. An analysis is made of performance differences in mathematics and science students in divergent systems. An overall conclusion is reached that the American comprehensive system more effectively serves all of the talent of a nation.

Nancy Karweit
  John Hopkins
  University
  Baltimore, Maryland

"Time on Task: A
Research Review"

88 pages

This report summarizes and evaluates existing studies of time use in schools. The first section describes theoretical views of time and learning. Two issues are discussed: the sources of variation in learning time (actual days per school year, length of school day, absenteeism), and the effects of learning time on achievement. In the second section, a review is presented of major empirical studies of time and learning, concentrating primarily on more recent studies of the effect of time on task. An analysis is given of the results of the Beginning Teacher Evaluation Study, as well as studies of: the effect of pupil attention on achievement; the relationship between concurrent achievement and attention measures; time allocation and achievement; and student response to different teaching methods. Inconsistent effects of time variables on achievement were found in the reviewed studies, and the conclusion is drawn that the effect of time on task on learning, while important, is not substantial. The final section discusses two elements which have been given scant attention in past studies of time on task: the conditioning effect of classroom/school organizational variables, and the dynamic nature of teaching and learning.

Howard London
  Bridgewater State
  College,
  Massachusetts

"Academic Standards
in the American
Community College:
Trends and
Controversies"

47 pages

Reasons for slipping academic standards in U.S. community colleges and a specific program combating this problem are discussed. Two reasons are offered for this slippage; the first has to do with the ambiguous state of the community college faculty. These teachers are said to have difficulty defining their roles because they feel a powerlessness in dealing with the college administration and in having to lower their standards for instruction and grading in dealing with their students. The second major reason for slippage given is the past and present trend toward student consumerism. The current reality of teachers having to resort to advertising for classes and schools having to advertise for easy programs is seen as having a detrimental effect on the attitudes of students and teachers. The vocational education emphasis that the community college has taken is traced, and arguments are offered for and against it. A program, established in two Florida community colleges, that has effectively raised academic standards is briefly described.

Martin L. Maehr
  University of Illinois,
  Champaign-Urbana

"Motivational Factors in School Achievement"

79 pages

A summary is presented of the literature on motivation relating to achievement in the classroom. Special attention is given to how values, ideology, and various cultural patterns may serve to enhance motivation to achieve in the classroom. In considering what determines motivation and personal investment in educational pursuits, the following factors are discussed: (1) individual personality; (2) teacher expectations; (3) dimensions of academic tasks; (4) sociocultural expectancies; and (5) family background and aspirations. Recent research on motivation and achievement provides discussion on the increasing emphasis being placed on judgments that the individual makes in relationship to perceived situations. Four components that figure prominently in motivation are discussed: (1) self-identity; (2) perceived autonomy and responsibility; (3) sense of direction; and (4) sense of competence. In the final section, certain conclusions are identified that may be useful in planning policy changes to improve schooling.

Matthew B. Miles
  Center for Policy
  Research
  New York, New York
Eleanor Farrar
Barbara Neufeld
  The Huron Institute
  Cambridge,
  Massachusetts

"The Extent of
Adoption of Effective
Schools Programs"

58 pages

A study was made of 39 secondary schools which had implemented new programs that had a research base in the effective
schools/classrooms literature, that were well-defined, and that
emphasized improvement effort at the building level. A discussion presenting the aims and methods of the study includes a
working definition of the effective schools programs and a
description of the sample schools' characteristics. Findings are
reported on: (1) characteristics of the districts and community
settings of the schools which adopted the new programs;
(2) program targets, goals, components, types, research bases,
and elementary-secondary differences; (3) timing and scope of
implementation, including length, funding sources, and costs;
and (4) types and degree of program impact, causative factors,
and implementation intentions. A summary of findings includes a discussion on the future of effective schools programs
in high schools. A list of programs and districts included in this
study is appended.

Barbara Neufeld
Eleanor Farrar
  The Huron Institute
  Cambridge,
  Massachusetts
Matthew B. Miles
  Center for Policy
  Research
  New York, New York

"A Review of Effective
Schools Research: The
Message for Secondary
Schools"

44 pages

A summary and critique is presented on research of effective
schools, based primarily on a review of the reviews written
about that work. It is pointed out that the majority of research
findings came from studies of elementary schools and focused
upon the characteristics of effective schools for minority and

poor students. Most research reviewed for this analysis was exploratory and descriptive, aiming to find effective schools and then deducing characteristics associated with effectiveness. For most studies reviewed, researchers did not develop comprehensive, systematic, and detailed programs with implementation guides for school improvement. However, in many studies, identification was made of features of effective programs. One example noted is of a school staff committed to excellence with high expectations for students and strong administrative leadership. It is suggested that the attitudes, processes, and techniques which characterize effective elementary schools have relevance for secondary schools as well, in spite of differences in organizational structure and educational goals. The appendix provides lists of effective school characteristics which were culled from the reviewed research.

William Neumann
Syracuse University,
New York

"College Press and
Student Fit"

30 pages

Six generalizations are offered regarding the collective requirements and expectations that colleges and universities impose on, or expect of, their students. (1) Colleges and universities in varying degrees expect and require students to demonstrate "basic academic skills" in reading, writing, and mathematics. Students must also learn how to adopt the professor's point of view. (2) Schools have given students considerable autonomy, thus expecting students to exhibit "self-sufficiency" with regard to managing time and to be able to learn through self-instruction. (3) Students must have a high level of "sociability" to get along with their peers as well as with the faculty. (4) Colleges and professors assume a certain and sustaining degree of "motivation"; professors do not feel it is their duty to interest the student. (5) Research indicates that those students with clearly defined goals and a sense of "direction" are more likely to persist and attain a college degree. (6) Colleges and universities require students to pay for their education; those students with "financial security" will study more effectively.

C. Robert Pace
  University of
  California,
  Los Angeles

"Achievement and
Quality of Student
Effort"

40 pages

This report is a comprehensive account of the accumulated research on the measurement of quality of effort and its significance in understanding the achievement of college students with regard to the College Student Experiences questionnaire (Pace, 1979). Results are based on the responses of 12,000 undergraduate students from 40 different colleges over a 3 year period. The questionnaire contained 14 quality of effort scales, on which students rated themselves on items concerned with the use of college facilities and the use of personal and social opportunities. The other parts of the questionnaire included items that enabled researchers to determine relationships between quality of effort and achievement and among many elements that might help to explain those relationships. A major conclusion of the study granted the importance of all elements that influence "who goes where" to college. The study also found that, once the students got to college, what counted most was not who they were or where they were but what they did. "Quality" effort appears to be what counts in achieving in college.

Harvey L. Prokop
  San Diego Unified
  School District
  California

"Intelligence, Motiva-
tion and the Quantity
and Quality of
Academic Work and
Their Impacts on the
Learning of Students:
A Practitioner's
Reaction"

17 pages

This paper analyzes the feasibility and likelihood of the implementations of recommendations in three papers: "Understanding Intelligence: What's in It for Educators?" (Robert J. Sternberg and Richard K. Wagner); "Motivating Students to Learn: A Lifelong Perspective" (Deborah J. Stipek); and "Academic Work" (Walter Doyle). Provided are summaries of all three papers and outlines of the major points which are either direct or indirect recommendations. Conclusions of the analysis include: (1) All three presentations do an "outstanding" job of summarizing the appropriate research and pointing educators in directions which the research seems to indicate; and (2) Many of the recommendations are characterized by less than precise directions of either what is to be done, or how such recommendations are to be implemented.

| Lauren B. Resnick University of Pittsburgh, Pennsylvania Daniel P. Resnick Carnegie-Mellon University Pittsburgh, Pennsylvania | "Standards, Curriculum, and Performance: An Historical and Comparative Perspective" | 53 pages |

The first section of this paper on educational standards considers the nature of the school curriculum as the shaper and delimiter of what is demanded of students. Debates over the desirability of a common or core curriculum for secondary schools as opposed to different programs are discussed. Demands for traditional academic disciplines and for vocational education and the way in which the changing needs of the labor market shape the school curriculum are examined. In the second section, tests and examinations as instruments of standard-setting are discussed. A distinction is made between those tests which monitor achievement but do not motivate or guide study, and those for which schools prepare students and which influence both the content and achievement levels of each course. The nearly complete absence of European-style examinations in American schools is documented and its implications for educational standards considered. Comparison is made between the American approach to student assessment and that of France and England. Suggestions are made in the final section on ways of improving standards in the American schools.

Frederick Rudolph Williams College Williamstown, Massachusetts	"Educational Excel- lence — The Secondary School-College Connec- tion and Other Matters: An Historical Assessment"	50 pages

For the first 200 years of American higher education, the baccalaurcate program was shaped by the authority of tradition, seldom challenged, and easily accommodating new learning and changing social conditions. After the Civil War, the authority of tradition was undermined by emerging professional academicians, trained in particular bodies of knowledge, and dedicated to a style of "scientific" learning. By World War II, tradition, professional academicians, and society shared authority over what went on in higher education. Since World War II, the accelerating democratization of higher education has created in students a new authority over their course of study. The evolution of the American college through these phases is traced in this paper. An analysis is presented of periods of American education, such as the beginnings of small provincial colleges in the eastern United States in the early 1800s, the growth of private and public universities in the late nineteenth century, and the development toward providing mass education immediately after World War II. Complex social changes that transformed secondary schools, colleges, and universities from their inception to the present are discussed in light of their influence on the thinking, attitudes, and aspirations of communities, students, teachers, and the government.

Clifford Sjogren University of Michigan, Ann Arbor	"College Admissions and the Transition to Postsecondary Education: Standards and Practices"	32 pages

In this review of college admission practices, four areas are analyzed: (1) changing patterns of admission standards and practices and factors that have influenced those changes during the past 25 years; (2) importance assigned to high school achievement, test scores, and other criteria in arriving at admission decisions; (3) influence of college admission standards and processes on high school curricula; and (4) practice of awarding college credit to students who are enrolled in high school. Following a description of the criteria that are generally used for individual admission decisions, an overview is presented of admission practices during each of four "eras" that fell within the period of 1957-81: (1) Sputnik Era (1957-60); (2) Post War Baby Boom Era (1964-67); (3) New Groups Era (1971-74); and (4) Stable Enrollment Era (1978-81). The paper concludes with a brief look at the immediate future. A bibliography is included.

Richard E. Snow **Stanford University,** **California**	**"Intelligence, Motivation and Academic Work" (A Critique of the Symposium on _The Student's Role in Learning_)**	**15 pages**

With respect to the high school student, there has been: (1) a decline over the past 10-15 years in high school student averages in aptitude for learning, in achievement from learning, and in motivation for further learning; (2) an increase in the need for remedial mathematics and reading and writing skill courses for college students; and (3) an even more severe need for remedial instruction for the non-college bound high school graduate, particularly in the military. In reviewing studies done on teenage reading and television viewing habits, it becomes obvious that many teenagers today show little purposive striving toward goals of intellectual development, and they invest little mental effort in learning. General observations of schools today indicate that they are profoundly diverse, porous, loosely-coupled systems and that the education system in general is panacea-ridden. These aspects of schools operate to complicate the problem and to thwart attempts at improvement. Recommendations for improvement include: (1) federal and state policies must be framed as adaptive strategies; (2) instructional strategies within a locale must be adaptive; (3) cognitive psychology needs to be researched more thoroughly; (4) cognitive instructional techniques must be taught to teachers; and (5) technology must be used in the classroom.

Robert J. Sternberg
Richard Wagner
  Yale University,
New Haven,
Connecticut

"Understanding
Intelligence: What's in
It for Educators?"

82 pages

This three-part report discusses the concept of intelligence and its importance for educators. Part 1 considers the basic question of what intelligence is. Part 2 discusses the implications of notions of intelligence for schooling, dealing with both the training of content knowledge and the training of intellectual skills. Each of these first two parts is divided into sections which discuss the psychometric view, the Piagetian view, the information-processing view, and comparison and evaluation of alternative approaches. Part 3 presents an outline of a program of instruction for intellectual skills, based upon a particular theory of intelligence. A bibliography is included.

Deborah Stipek
  University of
California,
  Los Angeles

"Motivating Students
to Learn: A Lifelong
Perspective"

56 pages

Two questions are addressed: (1) What are the motivational characteristics of a child who is most likely to achieve in school at an optimal level? and (2) What kind of educational environment fosters these characteristics? Evidence suggesting that external rewards and punishment can have negative long-term effects on achievement motivation is reviewed. A discussion is given of theoretical and empirical work demonstrating that it is not reinforcement per se that influences children's behavior, but beliefs about one's competencies, perceptions of the cause of achievement outcomes, and values regarding achievement-related rewards that determine behavior. For maintaining high motivation in children, the following strategies are recommended: (1) evaluating on a mastery rather than a normative standard; (2) minimizing salient public evidence of individual childrens' performance; (3) considering errors as a normal aspect of mastering new skills; and (4) providing opportunities for all children to demonstrate competence in activities valued by the teacher. Encouraging students to trust their own evaluations and to set reasonable goals and providing greater autonomy in learning situations are suggested to help them develop independent, self-directed learning strategies.

Judith Torney-Purta
  University of Mary-
  land, College Park
John Schwille
  Michigan State
  University,
  East Lansing

"The Values Learned   83 pages
in School: Policy and
Practice in Industrial-
ized Countries"

A comparative analysis of values education in the United States, Germany, Japan, Great Britain, the Soviet Union, Sweden, and Canada analyzed eight assertions: (1) No institution with education as its primary aim can be value neutral; (2) Countries differ in values which characterize their political cultures and in values which are taught in school; (3) None of the countries studied has had a uniformly high level of success in transmitting civic values; (4) The learning of values is strongly influenced by factors outside the school's control; (5) Educational policy has been somewhat effective in bringing about desired changes in values; (6) The learning of values in school is not limited to mandated programs of moral and civic education; (7) Several nations have developed curricular goals to promote common core values; and (8) Television and other mass media have an important and often negative effect on young people's values. It is recommended that coalition agenda be formed, providing a description of values that ought to be learned in school, together with the actions needed if these values are to be embodies in educational practice.

Beatrice Ward
John R. Mergendoller
Alexis L. Mitman
  Far West Laboratory
  for Educational
  Research and
  Development
  San Francisco,
  California

"The Years Between Elementary School and High School: What Schooling Experiences Do Students Have?"

51 pages

This paper discusses the modern American junior high and middle school from the perspectives of an interested observer, the educational researcher, and the students themselves. Discussed briefly are three factors that place junior high/middle school education in a unique context — the developmental stage of the students who are served, the historical rationale for creating such schools, and the current move to establish "middle" rather than "junior high" schools. Next, examples are provided of the ways teachers, students, and subjects are organized in these schools. This is followed by a discussion of the academic and social maturity requirements students must meet in order to perform successfully in junior high/middle schools. Also described are types of teaching practices that have been observed to be most effective at this educational level. Demands that are placed on students as they move from elementary to junior high/middle schools are summarized, as is a theme that runs throughout the paper, involving three aspects of a student's instructional program: (1) nature of academic tasks; (2) socio-organizational structure of the classroom; and (3) management and accountability systems employed by teachers.

Jonathan Warren
  Educational Testing
  Service
  Berkeley, California

"The Faculty Role in Educational Excellence"

55 pages

The high degree of autonomy college faculty members exercise in organizing and teaching courses suggests that faculty perceptions of educational purposes, subject matter structure and importance, and expectations for student learning are major determinants of educational success. Despite diversity and local autonomy present in its system, American higher education shows a substantial degree of coherence. Students and faculty move with reasonable ease from one institution to another. The autonomy of individual faculty members is countered by a complex network of influences: (1) prior educational and work experience and background characteristics; (2) textbooks and other instructional materials; (3) direct contact with other faculty members (e.g., curriculum committees, departmental discussions, informal contact); (4) professional literature; (5) professional associations and learned societies; and (6) the accreditation process. The first section of this paper describes the nature of the faculty network and its constraining influence on faculty teaching, educational content, and standards. The second section discusses how the effects of faculty views and expectations on student learning, as constrained by the existing system of influences, are or might be assessed. Procedures are described that would extend knowledge of the educational accomplishments of the higher education system while allowing for its diversity.

Dean K. Whitla   **"Value Added and**   **34 pages**
   Harvard University   **Other Related Matters"**
   Cambridge,
   Massachusetts

The term "value added" refers to the assessment of the amount of learning that takes place during the college years. Two experiments, Value Added I and Value Added II, attempted to measure college students' attainment of eight liberal education objectives: (1) writing ability; (2) analytical ability; (3) sensitivity to ethics, morals, and values; (4) mastery of concepts across major disciplines; (5) appreciation of self, social, and universal understanding; (6) interpersonal relationships; (7) view of life experiences; and (8) broad intellectual and aesthetic interests. Results from the Value Added I experiment demonstrated that change did occur during the college years, and results from Value Added II indicated that colleges can and do add value in very large and significant ways. Findings from these two studies are reflected upon as the author reviews past and current high school and college student trends, including Scholastic Aptitude Test scores, Achievement Test scores, sources of learning, and chosen vocations of graduates. Suggestions for improving the present state of American education are made.

Sam J. Yarger　　　　　**"Inservice Education"**　　**63 pages**
Syracuse University,
New York

This paper, on the state of inservice teacher education, is divided into five parts. The paper's first part, which focuses on the context in which teaching occurs and on the role of the teacher, points out that, while the common denominator in the study of teaching is the teacher/learner relationship, social issues also affect teachers and teaching. In the paper's second section, a profile is drawn of the current state of inservice education, including the magnitude of the endeavor, knowledge base, program content, program delivery, and evaluation. The third part of the paper gives examples of five high quality inservice programs and describes identified characteristics of effective inservice client involvement, recognition of district and school needs, focus on instruction of children, skill-driven training, and in-class observation, feedback, and coaching. In the fourth part, three main high level issues confronting education today are examined: the politicalization of inservice education, lack of institutional commitment, and the problem of incorporating inservice into the responsibilities of elementary and secondary teachers. The final section of the paper presents a recommendation for the founding of an American Education Congress. A brief discussion outlines the potential strengths of such a Congress in bringing about consensual policy setting and monitoring of education, specifically teacher education.

Herbert Zimiles
  Bank Street College
  of Education
  New York, New York

"The Changing Ameri-
can Child: The Perspec-
tive of Educators"

54 pages

A study was based on retrospective descriptions obtained from interviews with a large number of teachers who have taught for over 20 years. Three areas of change in students were consistently noted in the descriptions: children today know more, are freer, and grow up more rapidly. More autonomous, and armed with greater knowledge, children emerge from childhood more rapidly. Societal influences have had much impact on children, parents, teachers, and schooling. Television and other media have also consistently influenced children and schooling. Changes in the family structure, the relationship between parents and children, the increase in peer group influence, and in children's attitudes toward teachers and school are equally important. Educators today are faced with youngsters who, by the time they reach high school, have acquired many material possessions, been entertained and partially educated by the media, achieved a sophisticated degree of sexual awareness, and attained self-reliance by virtue of changes in the quality of family support. These young people, having achieved many visible features of adult status, find it difficult to think of themselves as needing still more preparation for life.

Chapter 4
Public Testimony

Many individuals outside the Commission contributed important commentary during a number of meetings, hearings, and other events. The schedule of these activities appears in Appendix D while hearing participants are listed in Appendix E. Summaries of testimony during the major hearings and panel discussions follow in chronological order.

Hearing: "Science, Mathematics, and Technology Education"
March 11, 1982
Stanford University, Stanford, California

A panel of seven Commission members, chaired by Glenn T. Seaborg, University Professor of Chemistry at the University of California, Berkeley, heard testimony before an audience of approximately 175 people. Five invited speakers presented national perspectives on the issues and responded to questions from the panel. Seventeen persons who had been invited in advance and eleven persons volunteering from the audience discussed regional programs and presented additional perspectives.

Testimony noted that science and technology have increasingly become the engine for change and progress in the quality of life, individual health, economic strength, and increasing opportunity. While we are still first in science and technology, we are being challenged by other nations. Meeting our national needs and remaining a strong international economic participant require first rate education in science, mathematics, and technology. Recent studies have shown that the United States is lagging Japan, West Germany, Eastern Europe, and Russia in the production of engineers and scientists. Other studies suggest a major offensive by the USSR to increase productivity and preparedness through science and engineering education.

Specific problems noted in U.S. science and mathematics education included the following:

○ Critical shortages of physics, mathematics, and chemistry teachers exist at the secondary level.

○ The average salary of a beginning math teacher with a bachelor's degree is now only 60% of the beginning salary offered by private industry to bachelor degree candidates in mathematics.

○ Substantial numbers of unqualified persons are teaching science and mathematics in secondary schools.

○ Even certified science and mathematics teachers at the secondary level are in need of in-service training.

○ New sequences of science and math courses and materials are needed which match stages of intellectual development of children.

○ Elementary and secondary schools need access to microcomputers, low-cost supplies, and other resources.

Hearing: "Language and Literacy"
April 16, 1982
Houston, Texas

A panel of five Commission members, chaired by Jay Sommer, foreign language teacher at New Rochelle High School in New York, and an audience of approximately 200 people heard testimony regarding the development of the higher-order language skills necessary for academic learning. Six invited speakers presented national perspectives on teaching reading, writing, and second languages and discussed related concerns with the Commission members. Sixteen other speakers presented their views on the hearing topics, predominantly from regional and local perspectives.

The general theme provided by the witnesses was that the language skills which should be emphasized in schools were the more sophisticated, integrated, concept-oriented skills of comprehension and composition. Each of the experts suggested that priority should be assigned to these high-level skills and that they can be taught through systematic instructional strategies requiring conscientious effort by teachers, administrators, and publishers. Special support of foreign language and bilingual education should continue. The presenters also agreed that to accomplish the task, adequate time must be allocated, possibly at the expense of other goals or activities.

Panel Discussion: "Performance Expectations in American Education"
April 30, 1982
Philadelphia, Pennsylvania

The Commission's first panel discussion focused on how expectations for student learning are formulated, whether they are compatible, whether they differ significantly from other countries, and what impact they have on student performance or on the behavior of schools and colleges. The panelists were chosen from four groups: employers in both the public and private sectors, college faculties and other academic societies, state agencies, and national independent educational organizations.

Themes that emerged included the following:

○ Expectations of excellence are determined by the particular viewpoint of who defines the standards. If, for example, examinations state expectations for learning, then those who write the examinations control the definition.

○ The degree of generality in the statement of educational objectives varies in direct proportion to the distance from the classroom of the person who is stating the objectives. The more general the statement of objectives, the more difficult it is to translate them into curriculum.

○ The very formulation of educational standards in terms of time spent on a subject (i.e., credits or units) may stand in the way of achieving excellence.

○ The anticipated enrollment decline at all levels of education has a negative effect on the motivations of educators to accept the implications of new and more precise statements of expectations.

○ The Commission may wish to consider the issue of raising the quality and demands of examinations currently in use through a more judicious balancing of essay and objective questions.

○ There is a need of increased cooperation, not merely between secondary and postsecondary institutions, but also between educational institutions and employers of all kinds.

Hearing: "Teaching and Teacher Education"
May 12, 1982
Georgia State University, Atlanta, Georgia

Testimony was heard from twenty-three individuals covering national, regional, and local perspectives. Observations focused on the need to resolve current and prospective teacher shortages as well as the uneven level of teaching quality across the country. Two areas for change were emphasized: recruiting and retaining qualified teachers and teacher training.

Teaching is facing serious difficulties in recruiting and retaining high-caliber college graduates. Teaching has historically attracted those who score below average among college graduates on tests of achievement, but this trend has intensified in recent years. Both the number and quality of those entering are declining. Teaching suffers from low salaries, the absence of a staged career and opportunities for advancement, and low prestige. Expanded professional opportunities have decreased teaching's relative attractiveness for women and minorities. Some evidence indicates that the intrinsic rewards derived from students are harder to come by in many schools. Other than compensation improvements, recommendations include scholarship and loan forgiveness programs, differentiated career paths, and mid-career internships for teachers with business and industry. Testing and certification of teachers can screen out those unqualified to teach while enhancing occupational prestige through increased standards.

Hearing participants gave several recommendations for teacher training: certification of education school faculty, more years of college education for teachers to accommodate more classroom experiences, required courses in all of the major curriculum areas, and increased funding of in-service training programs such as master teachers.

Hearing: "College admissions and the Transition to Postsecondary Education"
June 23, 1982
Chicago, Illinois

While the Commission engaged in a number of activities on its Chicago visit, the centerpiece was the public hearing. Both Commissioners and staff had hoped that the testimony and discussion at the hearing would probe a very complex set of factors and trends including the role of admissions in the strategic planning of colleges, the demands placed on post-secondary education by local economies and population groups, and student development in the transition process. It may be said, though, that the principal emphasis of the content of the hearing was on secondary schools and not colleges. The testimony implied that American colleges and universities are doing a fine job and are not facing any problems relevant to the concerns of the Commission other than poorly prepared high school students.

The major themes that stood out during the Chicago visit included the following:

○ Education has a significant and complex relationship to our national purpose.

○ College admission policies and practices that rely on formulas can *not* play a significant role in the enhancement of educational excellence.

○ Honors, advanced placement, and other "college level" programs offered in high school have more value in terms of both enriching the education of individuals and setting high standards for schools than they do in the chase for credentials.

○ The role of guidance and advisement is critical to both challenging students and encouraging them to maximize their options at all levels of education.

○ Educators remain divided over the comparative virtues of aptitude and achievement tests, but generally agree that the kind of tests we use sends important signals to both students and teachers.

○ The transition from secondary to postsecondary education is an extraordinarily complex process through which students search for both academic and personal identity but are woefully ignorant of the grounds of their choices.

Panel Discussion: "College Curriculum: Shape, Influence, and Assessment"
August 27, 1982
University of Rhode Island, Kingston, Rhode Island

The meeting was attended by an extraordinarily active audience of over 80 educators and citizens from four states. The audience also included representatives of such national organizations as the American Council on Education, the American Association of Colleges, and the College Board, and of such federal agencies as the Fund for the Improvement of Postsecondary Education, the National Endowment for the Humanities, the National Center for Education Statistics, and the Office of Postsecondary Education.

Findings from the panel discussion included the following:

o The quality of undergraduate teaching is far more important than the precise content of curriculum in the search for excellence.

o Within the precise content of curriculum, controlled diversity is highly desirable.

o Changes in the course offerings and the shape of general education requirements in colleges do, in fact, influence what high schools offer and what high school students take.

o Personal service courses, whether offered in high schools or colleges, may have limited utility for some students, but do not challenge the majority.

o Institutions of higher education have a particular responsibility to display ethical behavior and to uphold both public and academic values.

- The credit system does not present a magical formula that certifies what students have actually learned, but we have to find constructive ways of living with it.

- Integrative (or "synthetic") thinking is the most difficult form of thought for college students to master, yet most colleges have given little consideration to advancing synthethic thinking in the curriculum.

- Creative uses of assessment are keys to helping college faculty and administrators improve the quality of higher education and to clarifying the meaning of college degrees.

Hearing: "Education for the Gifted and Talented" October 15, 1982 Harvard University, Cambridge, Massachusetts

The hearing was attended by six commissioners plus the hearing chairman William Baker, retired Chairman of Bell Laboratories. Eight witnesses were invited to deliver formal testimony. 250 members of the public attended the hearing. The hearing attempted to define the "gifted" student and suggest programs to serve such individuals.

Recommendations offered to the Commission ranged over a number of areas. Some participants advocated ongoing research to refine our understanding of giftedness and how to select and nurture the gifted. Others said it is time to better apply what we already know. Many advocated formal efforts to develop programming for the gifted across grade levels and to place gifted activities at a high priority. Witnesses called for devices for giving public recognition to students with high achievement.

Chapter 5
Findings

We conclude that declines in educational performance are in large part the result of disturbing inadequacies in the way the educational process itself is often conducted. The findings that follow, culled from a much more extensive list, reflect four important aspects of the educational process: content, expectations, time, and teaching.

Findings Regarding Content

By content we mean the very "stuff" of education, the curriculum. Because of our concern about the curriculum, the Commission examined patterns of courses high school students took in 1964-69 compared with course patterns in 1976-81. On the basis of these analyses we conclude:

○ Secondary school curricula have been homogenized, diluted, and diffused to the point that they no longer have a central purpose. In effect, we have a cafeteria-style curriculum in which the appetizers and desserts can easily be mistaken for the main courses. Students have migrated from vocational and college preparatory programs to "general track" courses in large numbers. The proportion of students taking a general program of study has increased from 12 percent in 1964 to 42 percent in 1979.

○ This curricular smorgasbord, combined with extensive student choice, explains a great deal about where we find ourselves today. We offer intermediate algebra, but only 31 percent of our recent high school graduates complete it; we offer French I, but only 13 percent complete it; and we offer geography, but only 16 percent complete it. Calculus is available in schools enrolling about 60 percent of all students, but only 6 percent of all students complete it.

○ Twenty-five percent of the credits earned by general track high school students are in physical and health education, work experience outside the school, remedial English and mathematics, and personal service and development courses, such as training for adulthood and marriage.

Findings Regarding Expectations

We define expectations in terms of the level of knowledge, abilities, and skills school and college graduates should possess. They also refer to the time, hard work, behavior, self-discipline, and motivation that are essential for high student achievement. Such expectations are expressed to students in several different ways:

○ by grades, which reflect the degree to which students demonstrate their mastery of subject matter;

○ through high school and college graduation requirements, which tell students which subjects are most important;

○ by the presence or absence of rigorous examinations requiring students to demonstrate their mastery of content and skill before receiving a diploma or a degree;

○ by college admissions requirements, which reinforce high school standards; and

○ by the difficulty of the subject matter students confront in their texts and assigned readings.

Our analyses in each of these areas indicate notable deficiencies:

○ The amount of homework for high school seniors has decreased (two-thirds report less than 1 hour a night) and grades have risen as average student achievement has been declining.

○ In many other industrialized nations, courses in mathematics (other than arithmetic or general mathematics), biology, chemistry, physics, and geography start in grade 6 and are required of *all* students. The time spent on these subjects, based on class hours, is about three times that spent by even the most science-oriented U.S. students, i.e., those who select 4 years of science and mathematics in secondary school.

○ A 1980 State-by-State survey of high school diploma requirements reveals that only eight States require high schools to offer foreign language instruction, but none requires students to take the courses. Thirty-five States require only 1 year of mathematics, and 36 require only 1 year of science for a diploma.

○ In 13 States, 50 percent or more of the units required for high school graduation may be electives chosen by the student. Given this freedom to choose the substance of half or more of their education, many students opt for less demanding personal service courses, such as bachelor living.

○ "Minimum competency" examinations (now required in 37 States) fall short of what is needed, as the "minimum" tends to become the "maximum," thus lowering educational standards for all.

○ One-fifth of all 4-year public colleges in the United States must accept every high school graduate within the State regardless of program followed or grades, thereby serving notice to high school students that they can expect to attend college even if they do not follow a demanding course of study in high school or perform well.

○ About 23 percent of our more selective colleges and universities reported that their general level of selectivity declined during the 1970s, and 29 percent reported reducing the number of specific high school courses required for admission (usually by dropping foreign language requirements, which are now specified as a condition for admission by only one-fifth of our institutions of higher education).

○ Too few experienced teachers and scholars are involved in writing textbooks. During the past decade or so a large number of texts have been "written down" by their publishers to ever-lower reading levels in response to perceived market demands.

○ A recent study by Education Products Information Exchange revealed that a majority of students were able to master 80 percent of the material in some of their subject-matter texts before they had even opened the books. Many books do not challenge the students to whom they are assigned.

○ Expenditures for textbooks and other instructional materials have declined by 50 percent over the past 17 years. While some recommend a level of spending on texts of between 5 and 10 percent of the operating costs of schools, the budgets for basal texts and related materials have been dropping during the past decade and a half to only 0.7 percent today.

Findings Regarding Time
Evidence presented to the Commission demonstrates three disturbing facts about the use that American schools and students make of time: (1) compared to other nations, American

students spend much less time on school work; (2) time spent in the classroom and on homework is often used ineffectively; and (3) schools are not doing enough to help students develop either the study skills required to use time well or the willingness to spend more time on school work.

○ In England and other industrialized countries, it is not unusual for academic high school students to spend 8 hours a day at school, 220 days per year. In the United States, by contrast, the typical school day lasts 6 hours and the school year is 180 days.

○ In many schools, the time spent learning how to cook and drive counts as much toward a high school diploma as the time spent studying mathematics, English, chemistry, U.S. history, or biology.

○ A study of the school week in the United States found that some schools provided students only 17 hours of academic instruction during the week, and the average school provided about 22.

○ A California study of individual classrooms found that because of poor management of classroom time, some elementary students received only one-fifth of the instruction others received in reading comprehension.

○ In most schools, the teaching of study skills is haphazard and unplanned. Consequently, many students complete high school and enter college without disciplined and systematic study habits.

Findings Regarding Teaching
The Commission found that not enough of the academically able students are being attracted to teaching; that teacher preparation programs need substantial improvement; that the professional working life of teachers is on the whole unaccept-

able; and that a serious shortage of teachers exists in key fields.

- ○ Too many teachers are being drawn from the bottom quarter of graduating high school and college students.

- ○ The teacher preparation curriculum is weighted heavily with courses in "educational methods" at the expense of courses in subjects to be taught. A survey of 1,350 institutions training teachers indicated that 41 percent of the time of elementary school teacher candidates is spent in education courses, which reduces the amount of time available for subject matter courses.

- ○ The average salary after 12 years of teaching is only $17,000 per year (see Exhibit 4), and many teachers are required to supplement their income with part-time and summer employment. In addition, individual teachers have little influence in such critical professional decisions as, for example, textbook selection.

- ○ Despite widespread publicity about an overpopulation of teachers, severe shortages of certain kinds of teachers exist: in the fields of mathematics, science, and foreign languages; and among specialists in education for gifted and talented, language minority, and handicapped students.

- ○ The shortage of teachers in mathematics and science is particularly severe. A 1981 survey of 45 States revealed shortages of mathematics teachers in 43 States, critical shortages of earth sciences teachers in 33 States, and of physics teachers everywhere.

- ○ Half of the newly employed mathematics, science, and English teachers are not qualified to teach these subjects; fewer than one-third of U.S. high schools offer physics taught by qualified teachers.

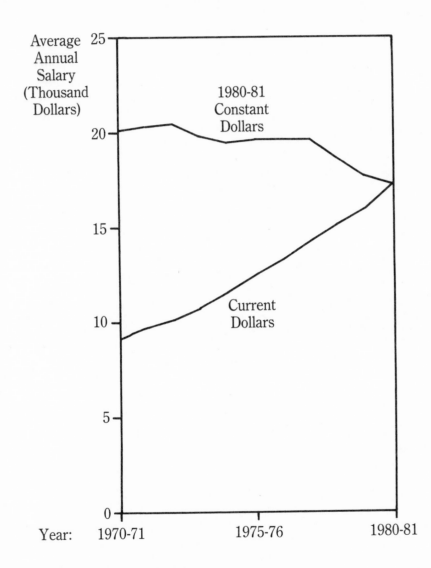

Exhibit 4
Average Annual Salaries of Classroom Teachers,
1970-71 to 1980-81

Average Annual Salary (Thousand Dollars)

1980-81 Constant Dollars

Current Dollars

Year: 1970-71   1975-76   1980-81

Source: National Education Association

Chapter 6
Recommendations

In light of the urgent need for improvement, both immediate and long term, this Commission has agreed on a set of recommendations that the American people can begin to act on now, that can be implemented over the next several years, and that promise lasting reform. The topics are familiar; there is little mystery about what we believe must be done. Many schools, districts, and States are already giving serious and constructive attention to these matters, even though their plans may differ from our recommendations in some details.

We wish to note that we refer to public, private, and parochial schools and colleges alike. All are valuable national resources. Examples of actions similar to those recommended below can be found in each of them.

We must emphasize that the variety of student aspirations, abilities, and preparation requires that appropriate content be available to satisfy diverse needs. Attention must be directed to both the nature of the content available and to the needs of particular learners. The most gifted students, for example, may need a curriculum enriched and accelerated beyond even the needs of other students of high ability. Similarly, educationally disadvantaged students may require special curriculum materials, smaller classes, or individual tutoring to help them master the material presented. Nevertheless, there remains a common expectation: We must demand the best effort and performance from all students, whether they are gifted or less able, affluent or disadvantaged, whether destined for college, the farm, or industry.

Our recommendations are based on the beliefs that everyone can learn, that everyone is born with an *urge* to learn which can be nurtured, that a solid high school education is within the reach of virtually all, and that life-long learning will equip people with the skills required for new careers and for citizenship.

Recommendation A: Content

We recommend *that State and local high school graduation requirements be strengthened and that,* at a minimum, all *students seeking a diploma be required to lay the foundations in the Five New Basics by taking the following curriculum during their 4 years of high school: (a) 4 years of English; (b) 3 years of mathematics; (c) 3 years of science; (d) 3 years of social studies; and (e) one-half year of computer science. For the college-bound, 2 years of foreign language in high school are strongly recommended in addition to those taken earlier.*

Whatever the student's educational or work objectives, knowledge of the New Basics is the foundation of success for the after-school years and, therefore, forms the core of the modern curriculum. A high level of shared education in these Basics, together with work in the fine and performing arts and foreign languages, constitutes the mind and spirit of our culture. The following Implementing Recommendations are intended as illustrative descriptions. They are included here to clarify what we mean by the essentials of a strong curriculum.

Implementing Recommendations

1. The teaching of *English* in high school should equip graduates to: (a) comprehend, interpret, evaluate, and use what they read; (b) write well-organized, effective papers; (c) listen effectively and discuss ideas intelligently; and (d) know our literary heritage and how it enhances imagination and ethical understanding, and how it relates to the customs, ideas, and values of today's life and culture.

2. The teaching of *mathematics* in high school should equip graduates to: (a) understand geometric and algebraic concepts; (b) understand elementary probability and statistics; (c) apply mathematics in everyday situations; and (d) estimate, approximate, measure, and test the accuracy of their calculations. In addition to the traditional sequence of studies available for college-bound students, new, equally demanding mathematics curricula need to be developed for those who do not plan to continue their formal education immediately.

3. The teaching of *science* in high school should provide graduates with an introduction to: (a) the concepts, laws, and processes of the physical and biological sciences; (b) the methods of scientific inquiry and reasoning; (c) the application of scientific knowledge to everyday life; and (d) the social and environmental implications of scientific and technological development. Science courses must be revised and updated for both the college-bound and those not intending to go to college. An example of such work is the American Chemical Society's "Chemistry in the Community" program.

4. The teaching of *social studies* in high school should be designed to: (a) enable students to fix their places and possibilities within the larger social and cultural structure; (b) understand the broad sweep of both ancient and contemporary ideas that have shaped our world; and (c) understand the fundamentals of how our economic system works and how our political system functions; and (d) grasp the difference between free and repressive societies. An understanding of each of these areas is requisite to the informed and committed exercise of citizenship in our free society.

5. The teaching of *computer science* in high school should equip graduates to: (a) understand the computer as an

information, computation, and communication device; (b) use the computer in the study of the other Basics and for personal and work-related purposes; and (c) understand the world of computers, electronics, and related technologies.

In addition to the New Basics, other important curriculum matters must be addressed.

6. Achieving proficiency in a *foreign language* ordinarily requires from 4 to 6 years of study and should, therefore, be started in the elementary grades. We believe it is desirable that students achieve such proficiency because study of a foreign language introduces students to non-English-speaking cultures, heightens awareness and comprehension of one's native tongue, and serves the Nation's needs in commerce, diplomacy, defense, and education.

7. The high school curriculum should also provide students with programs requiring rigorous effort in subjects that advance students' personal, educational, and occupational goals, such as the fine and performing arts and vocational education. These areas complement the New Basics, and they should demand the same level of performance as the Basics.

8. The curriculum in the crucial eight grades leading to the high school years should be specifically designed to provide a sound base for study in those and later years in such areas as English language development and writing, computational and problem solving skills, science, social studies, foreign language, and the arts. These years should foster an enthusiasm for learning and the development of the individual's gifts and talents.

9. We encourage the continuation of efforts by groups such as the American Chemical Society, the American

Association for the Advancement of Science, the Modern Language Association, and the National Councils of Teachers of English and Teachers of Mathematics, to revise, update, improve, and make available new and more diverse curricular materials. We applaud the consortia of educators and scientific, industrial, and scholarly societies that cooperate to improve the school curriculum.

Recommendation B: Standards and Expectations

We recommend *that schools, colleges, and universities adopt more rigorous and measurable standards, and higher expectations, for academic performance and student conduct, and that 4-year colleges and universities raise their requirements for admission. This will help students do their best educationally with challenging materials in an environment that supports learning and authentic accomplishment.*

Implementing Recommendations

1. Grades should be indicators of academic achievement so they can be relied on as evidence of a student's readiness for further study.

2. Four-year colleges and universities should raise their admissions requirements and advise all potential applicants of the standards for admission in terms of specific courses required, performance in these areas, and levels of achievement on standardized achievement tests in each of the five Basics and, where applicable, foreign languages.

3. Standardized tests of achievement (not to be confused with aptitude tests) should be administered at major transition points from one level of schooling to another

and particularly from high school to college or work. The purposes of these tests would be to: (a) certify the student's credentials; (b) identify the need for remedial intervention; and (c) identify the opportunity for advanced or accelerated work. The tests should be administered as part of a nationwide (but not Federal) system of State and local standardized tests. This system should include other diagnostic procedures that assist teachers and students to evaluate student progress.

4. Textbooks and other tools of learning and teaching should be upgraded and updated to assure more rigorous content. We call upon university scientists, scholars, and members of professional societies, in collaboration with master teachers, to help in this task, as they did in the post-Sputnik era. They should assist willing publishers in developing the products or publish their own alternatives where there are persistent in adequacies.

5. In considering textbooks for adoption, States and school districts should: (a) evaluate texts and other materials on their ability to present rigorous and challenging material clearly; and (b) require publishers to furnish evaluation data on the material's effectiveness.

6. Because no textbook in any subject can be geared to the needs of all students, funds should be made available to support text development in "thin-market" areas, such as those for disadvantaged students, the learning disabled, and the gifted and talented.

7. To assure quality, all publishers should furnish evidence of the quality and appropriateness of textbooks, based on results from field trials and credible evaluations. In view of the enormous numbers and varieties of texts available, more widespread consumer information services for purchasers are badly needed.

8. New instructional materials should reflect the most current applications of technology in appropriate curriculum areas, the best scholarship in each discipline, and research in learning and teaching.

Recommendation C: Time

We recommend *that significantly more time be devoted to learning the New Basics. This will require more effective use of the existing school day, a longer school day, or a lengthened school year.*

Implementing Recommendations

1. Students in high schools should be assigned far more homework than is now the case.

2. Instruction in effective study and work skills, which are essential if school and independent time is to be used efficiently, should be introduced in the early grades and continued throughout the student's schooling.

3. School districts and State legislatures should strongly consider 7-hour school days, as well as a 200- to 220-day school year.

4. The time available for learning should be expanded through better classroom management and organization of the school day. If necessary, additional time should be found to meet the special needs of slow learners, the gifted, and others who need more instructional diversity than can be accommodated during a conventional school day or school year.

5. The burden on teachers for maintaining discipline should be reduced through the development of firm and fair codes of student conduct that are enforced

consistently, and by considering alternative class-rooms, programs, and schools to meet the needs of continually disruptive students.

6. Attendance policies with clear incentives and sanctions should be used to reduce the amount of time lost through student absenteeism and tardiness.

7. Administrative burdens on the teacher and related intrusions into the school day should be reduced to add time for teaching and learning.

8. Placement and grouping of students, as well as promotion and graduation policies, should be guided by the academic progress of students and their instructional needs, rather than by rigid adherence to age.

Recommendation D: Teaching

This recommendation *consists of seven parts. Each is intended to improve the preparation of teachers or to make teaching a more rewarding and respected profession. Each of the seven stands on its own and should not be considered solely as an implementing recommendation.*

1. Persons preparing to teach should be required to meet high educational standards, to demonstrate an aptitude for teaching, and to demonstrate competence in an academic discipline. Colleges and universities offering teacher preparation programs should be judged by how well their graduates meet these criteria.

2. Salaries for the teaching profession should be increased and should be professionally competitive, market-sensitive, and performance-based. Salary, promotion, tenure, and retention decisions should be

tied to an effective evaluation system that includes peer review so that superior teachers can be rewarded, average ones encouraged, and poor ones either improved or terminated.

3. School boards should adopt an 11-month contract for teachers. This would ensure time for curriculum and professional development, programs for students with special needs, and a more adequate level of teacher compensation.

4. School boards, administrators, and teachers should cooperate to develop career ladders for teachers that distinguish among the beginning instructor, the experienced teacher, and the master teacher.

5. Substantial nonschool personnel resources should be employed to help solve the immediate problem of the shortage of mathematics and science teachers. Qualified individuals, including recent graduates with mathematics and science degrees, graduate students, and industrial and retired scientists could, with appropriate preparation, immediately begin teaching in these fields. A number of our leading science centers have the capacity to begin educating and retraining teachers immediately. Other areas of critical teacher need, such as English, must also be addressed.

6. Incentives, such as grants and loans, should be made available to attract outstanding students to the teaching profession, particularly in those areas of critical shortage.

7. Master teachers should be involved in designing teacher preparation programs and in supervising teachers during their probationary years.

Recommendation E: Leadership and Fiscal Support

We recommend *that citizens across the Nation hold educators and elected officials responsible for providing the leadership necessary to achieve these reforms, and that citizens provide the fiscal support and stability required to bring about the reforms we propose.*

Implementing Recommendations

1. Principals and superintendents must play a crucial leadership role in developing school and community support for the reforms we propose, and school boards must provide them with the professional development and other support required to carry out their leadership role effectively. The Commission stresses the distinction between leadership skills involving persuasion, setting goals and developing community consensus behind them, and managerial and supervisory skills. Although the latter are necessary, we believe that school boards must consciously develop leadership skills at the school and district levels if the reforms we propose are to be achieved.

2. State and local officials, including school board members, governors, and legislators, have *the primary responsibility* for financing and governing the schools, and should incorporate the reforms we propose in their educational policies and fiscal planning.

3. The Federal Government, in cooperation with States and localities, should help meet the needs of key groups of students such as the gifted and talented, the socioeconomically disadvantaged, minority and lan-

guage minority students, and the handicapped. In combination these groups include both national resources and the Nation's youth who are most at risk.

4. In addition, we believe the Federal Government's role includes several functions of national consequence that States and localities alone are unlikely to be able to meet: protecting constitutional and civil rights for students and school personnel; collecting data, statistics, and information about education generally; supporting curriculum improvement and research on teaching, learning, and the management of schools; supporting teacher training in areas of critical shortage or key national needs; and providing student financial assistance and research and graduate training. We believe the assistance of the Federal Government should be provided with a minimum of administrative burden and intrusiveness.

5. The Federal Government has *the primary responsibility* to identify the national interest in education. It should also help fund and support efforts to protect and promote that interest. It must provide the national leadership to ensure that the Nation's public and private resources are marshaled to address the issues discussed in this report.

6. This Commission calls upon educators, parents, and public officials at all levels to assist in bringing about the educational reform proposed in this report. We also call upon citizens to provide the financial support necessary to accomplish these purposes. Excellence costs. But in the long run mediocrity costs far more.

Chapter 7
Call to Action

Despite the obstacles and difficulties that inhibit the pursuit of superior educational attainment, we are confident, with history as our guide, that we can meet our goal. The American educational system has responded to previous challenges with remarkable success. In the 19th century our land-grant colleges and universities provided the research and training that developed our Nation's natural resources and the rich agricultural bounty of the American farm. From the late 1800s through mid-20th century, American schools provided the educated workforce needed to seal the success of the Industrial Revolution and to provide the margin of victory in two world wars. In the early part of this century and continuing to this very day, our schools have absorbed vast waves of immigrants and educated them and their children to productive citizenship. Similarly, the Nation's Black colleges have provided opportunity and undergraduate education to the vast majority of college-educated Black Americans.

More recently, our institutions of higher education have provided the scientists and skilled technicians who helped us transcend the boundaries of our planet. In the last 30 years, the schools have been a major vehicle for expanded social opportunity, and now graduate 75 percent of our young people from high school. Indeed, the proportion of Americans of college age enrolled in higher education is nearly twice that of Japan and far exceeds other nations such as France, West Germany, and the Soviet Union. Moreover, when international comparisons were last made a decade ago, the top 9 percent of American students compared favorably in achievement with their peers in other countries.

In addition, many large urban areas in recent years report that average student achievement in elementary schools is improving. More and more schools are also offering advanced placement programs and programs for gifted and talented students, and more and more students are enrolling in them.

We are the inheritors of a past that gives us every reason to believe that we will succeed.

A Word to Parents and Students

The task of assuring the success of our recommendations does not fall to the schools and colleges alone. Obviously, faculty members and administrators, along with policymakers and the mass media, will play a crucial role in the reform of the educational system. But even more important is the role of parents and students, and to them we speak directly.

To Parents
You know that you cannot confidently launch your children into today's world unless they are of strong character and well-educated in the use of language, science, and mathematics. They must possess a deep respect for intelligence, achievement, and learning, and the skills needed to use them; for setting goals; and for disciplined work. That respect must be accompanied by an intolerance for the shoddy and second-rate masquerading as "good enough."

You have the right to demand for your children the best our schools and colleges can provide. Your vigilance and your refusal to be satisfied with less than the best are the imperative first step. But your right to a proper education for your children carries a double responsibility. As surely as you are your child's first and most influential teacher, your child's ideas about education and its significance begin with you. You must be a *living* example of what you expect your children to honor and to emulate. Moreover, you bear a responsibility to participate actively in your child's education. You should encourage more diligent study and discourage satisfaction with mediocrity and the attitude that says "let it slide"; monitor your child's study; encourage good study habits; encourage your child to take more demanding rather than less demanding courses; nurture your child's curiosity, creativity, and confidence; and be an active participant in the work of the schools. Above all, exhibit a commitment to continued learning in your own life. Finally, help your children understand that excellence in education cannot be achieved without intellectual and moral integrity coupled with hard work and commitment. Children will look to their parents and teachers as models of such virtues.

To Students
You forfeit your chance for life at its fullest when you withhold your best effort in learning. When you give only the minimum to learning, you receive only the minimum in return. Even with your parents' best example and your teachers' best efforts, in the end it is *your* work that determines how much and how well you learn. When you work to your full capacity, you can hope to attain the knowledge and skills that will enable you to create your future and control your destiny. If you do not, you will have your future thrust upon you by others. Take hold of your life, apply your gifts and talents, work with dedication and self-discipline. Have high expectations for yourself and convert every challenge into an opportunity.

A Final Word

This is not the first or only commission on education, and some of our findings are surely not new, but old business that now at last must be done. For no one can doubt that the United States is under challenge from many quarters.

Children born today can expect to graduate from high school in the year 2000. We dedicate our report not only to these children, but also to those now in school and others to come. We firmly believe that a movement of America's schools in the direction called for by our recommendations will prepare these children for far more effective lives in a far stronger America.

Our final word, perhaps better characterized as a plea, is that all segments of our population give attention to the implementation of our recommendations. Our present plight did not appear overnight, and the responsibility for our current situation is widespread. Reform of our educational system will take time and unwavering commitment. It will require equally widespread, energetic, and dedicated action. For example, we call upon the National Academy of Sciences, National Academy of Engineering, Institute of Medicine, Science Service, National Science Foundation, Social Science Research Council, American Council of Learned Societies, National Endowment for the Humanities, National Endowment for the Arts, and other scholarly, scientific, and learned societies for their help in this effort. Help should come from students themselves; from parents, teachers, and school boards; from colleges and universities; from local, State, and Federal officials; from teachers' and administrators' organizations; from industrial and labor councils; and from other groups with interest in and responsibility for educational reform.

It is their America, and the America of all of us, that is at risk; it is to each of us that this imperative is addressed. It is by our willingness to take up the challenge, and our resolve to see it through, that America's place in the world will be either secured or forfeited. Americans have succeeded before and so we shall again.

Appendices

Appendix A: Charter National Commission on Excellence in Education

Authority

20 U.S.C. 1233a. The Commission is governed by the provisions of Part D of the General Education Provisions Act (P.L. 90-247 as amended; 20 U.S.C. 1233 *et seq.*) and the Federal Advisory Committee Act (P.L. 92-463; 5 U.S.C Appendix I) which set forth standards for the formation and use of advisory committees.

Purpose and Functions

The Commission advises and makes recommendations to the nation and to the Secretary of Education. To carry out this mission the Commission is charged with the following responsibilities:

(1) To review and synthesize the data and scholarly literature on the quality of learning and teaching in the nation's schools, colleges, and universities, both public and private, with special concern for the educational experience of teen-age youth;

(2) To examine and to compare and contrast the curricula, standards, and expectations of the educational systems of several advanced countries with those of the United States;

(3) To study a representative sampling of university and college admission standards and lower division course requirements with particular reference to the impact upon the enhancement of quality and the promotion of excellence such standards may have on high school curricula and on expected levels of high school academic achievement;

(4) To review and to describe educational programs that are recognized as preparing students who consistently attain higher than average scores in college entrance examinations and who meet with uncommon success the demands placed on them by the nation's colleges and universities;

(5) To review the major changes that have occurred in American education as well as events in society during the past quarter century that have significantly affected educational achievement;

(6) To hold hearings and to receive testimony and expert advice on efforts that could and should be taken to foster higher levels of quality and academic excellence in the nation's schools, colleges, and universities;

(7) To do all other things needed to define the problems of and the barriers to attaining greater levels of excellence in American education; and

(8) To report and to make practical recommendations for action to be taken by educators, public officials, governing boards, parents, and others having a vital interest in American education and a capacity to influence it for the better.

Structure

The Commission consists of at least 12, but not more than 19, public members appointed by the Secretary. The Secretary shall designate a chairperson from among the members. Among its members the Commission includes persons who are knowledgeable about educational programs at various levels and are familiar with views of the public, of employers, of educators, and of leaders of a range of professions regarding the status of education today, requirements for the future, and ways the quality of education for all Americans can be improved.

A quorum of the Commission is a majority of appointed members.

Terms of service of members end with the termination of the Commission.

Hearings on behalf of the Commission may be held by one or more members with the authorization of the chairperson.

The Commission may establish standing committees composed exclusively of its members. Each standing committee complies with the requirements of applicable statutes and Departmental regulations. Each committee presents to the Commission findings and recommendations for action by the full Commission. Timely notification of the establishment of a committee and any change therein, including its charge, membership, and frequency of meetings, will be made in writing to the Committee Management Officer. All committees act under the policies established by the Commission as a whole.

Management and staff services are provided by the Executive Director who serves as the Designated Federal Official to the Commission and by the National Institute of Education.

Meetings

The Commission meets approximately four times a year at the call of the Chairperson, with the advance approval of the Secretary or the Designated Federal Official who approves the agenda and is present or represented at all meetings. Standing committees meet as required at the call of their Chairperson with the concurrence of the Commission Chairperson. All meetings are open to the public except as determined otherwise by the Assistant Secretary for Educational Research and Improvement. Notice of all meetings shall be given to the public. Meetings are conducted, and records of proceedings kept, in accordance with applicable laws and Department regulations.

Compensation

In accordance with the General Education Provisions Act and other applicable laws, Commission members shall be entitled to an honorarium of $100 per day for official business of the Commission. Their per diem and travel expenses will be paid in accordance with Federal Travel Regulations.

Annual Cost Estimate

Estimate of the direct cost for operating the Commission, including compensation and travel expenses for members as well as costs for studies, but excluding staff support, is $332,000. Estimate of annual person-years of staff required is 16. Estimate of direct annual costs for administrative support, staff and staff per diem and travel expenses is $453,000. The National Institute of Education will provide additional administrative and research assistance to the Commission.

Reports

In addition to its final report, which is expected eighteen months from the initial meeting, the Commission submits to the Congress by March 31 of each year an annual report which contains as a minimum a list of the names and business addresses of the members, a list of the dates and places of the meetings, the functions of the Commission, and a summary of Commission activities and recommendations made during the year. Such report is transmitted with the Secretary's annual report to Congress. The Commission makes such other reports or recommendations as may be appropriate. A copy of the annual report and other reports is provided to the Committee Management Officer.

Termination Date

It is estimated that the time necessary for the Commission to complete its activities and report is at least 18 months. Therefore, to insure the completion of the report, the Secretary determines that this Commission terminates not later than two years from the date of this Charter.

APPROVED:

August 5, 1981

Date   Secretary

Appendix B: Members of the National Commission on Excellence in Education

David P. Gardner (Chair)
President
University of Utah and
President-Elect, University of California
Salt Lake City, Utah

Yvonne W. Larsen (Vice-Chair)
Immediate Past-President
San Diego City School Board
San Diego, California

William O. Baker
Chairman of the Board (Retired)
Bell Telephone Laboratories
Murray Hill, New Jersey

Anne Campbell
Former Commissioner of Education
State of Nebraska
Lincoln, Nebraska

Margaret S. Marston
Member
Virginia State Board of Education
Arlington, Virginia

Albert H. Quie
Former Governor
State of Minnesota
St. Paul, Minnesota

Francisco D. Sanchez, Jr.
Superintendent of Schools
Albuquerque Public Schools
Albuquerque, New Mexico

Glenn T. Seaborg
University Professor of Chemistry
and Nobel Laureate
University of California
Berkeley, California

Jay Sommer
National Teacher of the Year, 1981-82
Foreign Language Department
New Rochelle High School
New Rochelle, New York

Richard Wallace
Principal
Lutheran High School East
Cleveland Heights, Ohio

Emeral A. Crosby
Principal
Northern High School
Detroit, Michigan

Charles A. Foster, Jr.
Immediate Past-President
Foundation for Teaching Economics
San Francisco, California

Norman C. Francis
President
Xavier University of Louisiana
New Orleans, Louisiana

A. Bartlett Giamatti
President
Yale University
New Haven, Connecticut

Appendix C: Letter of Transmittal of the Study

Honorable T. H. Bell   April 26, 1983
Secretary of Education
U.S. Department of Education
Washington, D.C. 20202

Dear Mr. Secretary:

On August 26, 1981, you created the National Commission on Excellence in Education
and directed it to present a report on the quality of education in America to you and to the
American people by April of 1983.

It has been my privilege to chair this endeavor and on behalf of the members of the
Commission it is my pleasure to transmit this report, *A Nation at Risk: The Imperative
for Educational Reform.*

Our purpose has been to help define the problems afflicting American education and to
provide solutions, not search for scapegoats. We addressed the main issues as we saw
them, but have not attempted to treat the subordinate matters in any detail. We were
forthright in our discussions and have been candid in our report regarding both the
strengths and weaknesses of American education.

The Commission deeply believes that the problems we have discerned in American
education can be both understood and corrected if the people of our country, together
with those who have public responsibility in the matter, care enough and are courageous
enough to do what is required.

Each member of the Commission appreciates your leadership in having asked this diverse
group of persons to examine one of the central issues which will define our Nation's
future. We especially welcomed your confidence throughout the course of our
deliberations and your anticipation of a report free of political partisanship.

It is our collective and earnest hope that you will continue to provide leadership in this
effort by assuring wide dissemination and full discussion of this report, and by encouraging
appropriate action throughout the country. We believe that materials compiled by the
Commission in the course of its work constitute a major resource for all persons
interested in American education.

The other Commissioners and I sincerely appreciate the opportunity to have served our
country as members of the National Commission on Excellence in Education, and on their
behalf I remain,

Respectfully,

David Pierpont Gardner
Chairman

Appendix D: Schedule of the Commission's Public Events

Event	Date(s)	Place
Full Commission Meeting	October 9-10, 1981	Washington, D.C.
Full Commission Meeting	December 7, 1981	Washington, D.C.
Full Commission Meeting	February 25, 1982	Washington, D.C.
Hearing—Science, Mathematics, and Technology Education	March 11, 1982	Stanford University Stanford, California
Hearing—Language and Literacy: Skills for Academic Learning	April 16, 1982	Houston Independent School District Houston, Texas
Panel Discussion—Performance Expectations in American Education	April 30, 1982	The University of Pennsylvania Philadelphia, Pennsylvania
Hearing—Teaching and Teacher Education	May 12, 1982	Georgia State University Atlanta, Georgia
Full Commission Meeting	May 25, 1982	Washington, D.C.
Hearing—College Admissions and the Transition to Post-secondary Education	June 23, 1982	Roosevelt University Chicago, Illinois
Symposium—The Student's Role in Learning	July 30, 1982	San Diego State University California

Event	Date(s)	Place
Panel Discussion— College Curriculum: Shape, Influence, and Assessment	August 27, 1982	University of Rhode Island Kingston, Rhode Island
Hearing—Education for a Productive Role in a Productive Society	September 16, 1982	St. Cajetan's Center Denver, Colorado
Full Commission Meeting	September 28-29, 1982	New York, New York
Hearing—Education for the Gifted and Talented	October 15, 1982	Harvard University Cambridge, Massachusetts
Full Commission Meeting	November 15-16, 1982	Washington, D.C.
Full Commission Meeting	January 21-22, 1983	Washington, D.C.
Full Commission Meeting	April 26, 1983	Washington, D.C.

Appendix E: Hearing Participants and Related Activities

Science, Mathematics, and Technology Education

H. Guyford Stever, National Academy of Sciences, Washington, D.C.

Bernard M. Oliver, Hewlett-Packard Company, Palo Alto, California

Henry L. Alder, University of California, Davis, representing the Council of Scientific Society Presidents

Sarah E. Klein, Roton Middle School, Norwalk, Connecticut, representing the National Science Teachers Association

Harold D. Taylor, Hillsdale High School, San Mateo, California, representing the National Council of Teachers of Mathematics

---

John Martin, Palo Alto Unified School District, California

Ruth Willis, Hamilton Junior High School, Oakland, California

Sam Dederian, San Francisco Unified School District, California

Leroy Finkel, San Mateo County Office of Education, California

Olivia Martinez, San Jose Unified School District, California

Robert Bell, General Electric Company, San Jose, California

Judith Hubner, representing the Governor's Office, State of California

Robert W. Walker, De Anza-Foothill Community College District, California

Nancy Kreinberg, Lawrence Hall of Science, Berkeley, California

Robert Finnell, Lawrence Hall of Science, Berkeley, California

Marian E. Koshland, University of California, Berkeley, representing the National Science Board

Alan M. Portis, University of California, Berkeley, representing the Education Committee of the American Physical Society

Leon Henkin, University of California, Berkeley, representing the U.S. Commission on Mathematical Instruction

John Pawson, Edison High School, Huntington Beach, California

Alan Fibish, Lowell High School, San Francisco, California

Juliet R. Henry, representing the California Teachers Association

Jess Bravin, Board of Education, Los Angeles, California

Frank Oppenheimer, Exploratorium, San Francisco, California
Leigh Burstein, University of California, Los Angeles
Judy Chamberlain, Cupertino Unified School District, California
Michael Summerville, Fremont Unified High School District, California
Ted Perry, San Juan Unified School District, California
Paul DeHart Hurd, Stanford University, California
Elizabeth Karplus, Campolindo High School, Moraga, California
Louis Fein, Palo Alto Learners Association, California
Bob McFarland, representing the California Math Council
Katherine Burt, Cupertino Elementary School District, California
Leo Ruth, California Engineering Foundation

Gordon M. Ambach, State Education Department, Albany, New York
James L. Casey, State Department of Education, Oklahoma City,
    Oklahoma
Carolyn Graham, Jefferson Elementary School, Burbank, California
Marcy Holteen, Ambler, Pennsylvania
Howard C. Mel and Kay Fairwell, Lawrence Hall of Science, Berkeley,
    California
Jean Phillips, Thousand Oaks, California
Simon Ramo, the TRW-Fujitsu Company, Redondo Beach, California
Gerhardt W. Reidel, University of West Los Angeles, Culver City,
    California
Carl L. Riehm, Virginia State Department of Education, Richmond,
    Virginia
John H. Saxon, Norman, Oklahoma
Thomas O. Sidebottom, Interactive Sciences, Inc., Palo Alto, California
Karl Weiss, Northeastern University, Boston, Massachusetts
Jan West, Oroville, California

Related Activities in the Bay Area

Site Visit
        Lawrence Hall of Science
        University of California, Berkeley
        Howard C. Mel, Director
Tour of the Paul and Jean Hanna Collection on the Role of Education and
        the Archives and Library at the Hoover Institution, Stanford
        University
Dinner with business, education, and community leaders
        Sponsored by the Chamber of Commerce of the United
        States, Western Regional Office, and the William and Flora
        Hewlett Foundation

Language and Literacy: Skills for Academic Learning

Richard C. Anderson, University of Illinois, Champaign-Urbana
Margaret Smith-Burke, New York University, New York
Donald Graves, University of New Hampshire, Durham
Eileen Lundy, University of Texas, San Antonio
Ray Clifford, Defense Language Institute, Presidio of Monterey, California
Lily Wong-Fillmore, University of California, Berkeley

Victoria Bergin, Texas Education Agency, Austin
Alan C. Purves, University of Illinois, Champaign-Urbana
Delia Pompa, Houston Independent School District, Texas
Olivia Munoz, Houston Independent School District, Texas
James Kinneavy, University of Texas, Austin
Betty Von Maszewski, Deer Park Independent School District, Texas
Claire E. Weinstein, University of Texas, Austin
Patricia Sturdivant, Houston Independent School District, Texas

June Dempsey, University of Houston, Texas, representing the American Association of Community and Junior Colleges, the Western College Reading Association, and the National Association for Remedial and Developmental Studies in Postsecondary Education
Jane Porter, College Board, Austin, Texas
Kay Bell, Texas Classroom Teachers Association, Austin, Texas
Judy Walker de Felix, University of Houston, Texas
Barbara Glave, University of Houston, Texas, representing the Houston Area Teachers of Foreign Language
Dora Scott, Houston Independent School District, Texas, representing the National Education Association and the Texas State Teachers Association, Houston
Georgette Sullins, Spring Independent School District, Texas
Renate Donovan, Spring Branch Independent School District, Texas

Gordon M. Ambach, State Education Department, Albany, New York
Jo Bennett and Jean Parochetti, Alvin Community College, Texas
Sharon Robinson, National Education Association, Washington, D.C.
Donald L. Rubin, University of Georgia, Athens, representing the Speech Communication Association
Robert N. Schwartz, University of Houston, Texas
Ralph C. Staiger, International Reading Association, Newark, Delaware

Helen Warriner-Burke and Carl L. Riehm, Department of Education, Richmond, Virginia

William Work, Speech Communication Association, Annandale, Virginia

Daryl R. Yost, East Allen County Schools, New Haven, Indiana

Related Activities in Houston

Site visits coordinated by the Office of the General Superintendent of the Houston Independent School District

> Briargrove Elementary School
> Wilson Elementary School
> Clifton Middle School
> Bellaire High School
> High School for Engineering Professions
> High School for Health Professions
> High School for Performing and Visual Arts

Teaching and Teacher Education

Gary Sykes, National Institute of Education, Washington, D.C.

Gary Fenstermacher, Virginia Polytechnic Institute and State University, Blacksburg

David G. Imig, American Association of Colleges for Teacher Education, Washington, D.C.

Anne Flowers, Georgia Southern University, Statesboro

Barbara Peterson, Seven Oaks Elementary School, Columbia, South Carolina

Eva Galumbos, Southern Regional Education Board, Atlanta, Georgia

Robert Scanlon, Pennsylvania State Department of Education, Harrisburg

Ralph Turlington, Florida State Department of Education, Tallahassee

Gail MacColl, National Institute of Education, Washington, D.C.

Kathy Jones, Roan State Community College, Harriman, Tennessee, representing the National Education Association

Mary Lou Romaine, Atlanta Federation of Teachers, Georgia, representing the American Federation of Teachers

Janet Towslee-Collier, Georgia State University, Atlanta, representing the Association of Teacher Educators

Robert Fortenberry, Jackson City Schools, Mississippi, representing the American Association of School Administrators

Nicholas Hobar, West Virginia Department of Education, Charleston, representing the National Association of State Directors of Teacher Education and Certification

Fred Loveday, Georgia Private Education Council, Smyrna, representing the Council for American Private Education

James Lowden, Alabama Christian Education Association, Prattville, representing the American Association of Christian Schools

J.L. Grant, Florida State University, Tallahassee, representing the American Association for Colleges of Teacher Education

Carolyn Huseman, Georgia State Board of Education, representing the National Association of State Boards of Education

---

Robert Fontenot, University of Southwestern Louisiana, LaFayette

Nancy Ramseur, Camden High School, South Carolina

Eugene Kelly, George Washington University, Washington, D.C.

Richard Hodges, Decatur, Georgia

James Gray, University of California, Berkeley

Robert Dixon, Institute for Research, Development and Engineering in Nuclear Energy, Atlanta, Georgia

Pat Woodall, Columbus, Georgia

Wayne Wheatley, Furman University, Greenville, South Carolina, representing the Council for Exceptional Children

Joe Hasenstab, Project Teach, Westwood, New Jersey

William Drummond, University of Florida, Gainesville

Debbie Yoho, Southeastern Regional Teacher Center, Columbia, South Carolina

Donald Gallehr, Virginia Writing Project, Fairfax

James Collins, National Council of States on In-service Education, Syracuse, New York

Ann Levy, Project New Adventure in Learning, Tallahassee, Florida

Bill Katzenmeyer, University of South Florida, Tampa

Walt Mika, Virginia Education Association

Eunice Sims, Georgia Writing Project, Atlanta

Gordon M. Ambach, State Education Department, Albany, New York

Elaine Banks and Sam Sava, National Association of Elementary School Principals, Reston, Virginia

Aladino A. Burchianti, Masontown, Pennsylvania

Roy Edelfelt, Washington, D.C.

Ed Foglia, California Teachers Association, Burlingame

June Johnson, New Adventure in Learning, Tallahassee, Florida

Richard A. Krueger, Staples Teacher Center, Minnesota

Clare Miezio, Eagle Forum Education Committee, Schaumburg, Illinois

Donald L. Rubin, University of Georgia, Athens, representing the
Speech Communication Association Committee on Assessment and
Testing
Daryl R. Yost, East Allen County Schools, New Haven, Indiana

Related Activities in Atlanta

Site Visits
Douglas High School
L.W. Butts, Principal
Mays High School
Thomas E. Wood, Jr., Principal

Lunch with local dignitaries hosted by Georgia State University

Dinner with business, education, and community leaders
Coordinated by the Atlanta Partnership of Business and Education
Sponsored by FABRAP Architects, Inc., and the Coca-Cola
Company

College Admissions and the Transition to Postsecondary Education
Clifford Sjogren, University of Michigan, Ann Arbor
Ralph McGee, New Trier Township High School, Winnetka, Illinois
Alice Cox, University of California Systemwide Administration, Berkeley
George Stafford, Prairie View A&M University, Texas
Fred Hargadon, Stanford University, California
Margaret MacVicar, Massachusetts Institute of Technology, Cambridge

Lois Mazzuca, National Association of College Admissions Counselors,
Rolling Meadows, Illinois
Ora McConnor, Chicago Public Schools, Illinois
Theodore Brown, Hales Franciscan High School, Chicago, Illinois
Charles D. O'Connell, University of Chicago, Illinois
Oscar Shabat, Chicago Community College System, Illinois
Arnold Mitchum, Marquette University, Milwaukee, Wisconsin
Michael Kean, Educational Testing Service, Midwestern Regional Office, Evanston, Illinois

John B. Vaccaro, The College Board, Midwestern Regional Office,
Evanston, Illinois
William Kinnison, Wittenberg University, Springfield, Ohio

William J. Pappas, Northview High School, Grand Rapids, Michigan
Carmelo Rodriguez, ASPIRA of Illinois, Chicago
Jeffrey Mallow, Loyola University, Chicago, Illinois
Carol Elder, Local 4100 of American Federation of Teachers, Chicago,
Illinois
Bettye J. Lewis, Michigan Alliance of Families
Rachel Ralya, Michigan Alliance of Families
Austin Doherty, Alverno College, Milwaukee, Wisconsin

Gordon M. Ambach, State Education Department, Albany, New York
Gordon C. Godbey, Pennsylvania Association for Adult Continuing Education
cation
Daryl R. Yost, East Allen County Schools, New Haven, Indiana

Related Activities in Chicago
Site Visits
> Standard Oil of Indiana
>> Gene E. Cartwright, Manager of Employee Relations
>> Joseph Feeney, Director, Training and Personnel
>> Planning

> Continental Illinois Bank
>> Jennifer Olsztynski, Personnel Manager
> De Paul University
>> Rev. John T. Richardson, President
>> David Justice, Dean, School for New Learning

Luncheon with leaders of higher education institutions
> Sponsored by the John D. and Catherine T. MacArthur Foundation
> tion

Dinner with business, education, and community leaders
> Sponsored by the John D. and Catherine T. MacArthur Foundation
> tion
> Chaired by Stanley O. Ikenberry, President, University of Illinois
> nois

Education for a Productive Role in a Productive Society

Daniel Saks, Brookings Institution, Washington, D.C.

Roy Forbes, Education Commission of the States, Denver, Colorado

Sol Hurwitz, Committee for Economic Development, New York, New York

Martha Brownlee, Naval Education and Training for Research and Development, Pensacola, Florida

Norman Pledger, Colorado AFL-CIO, Denver

Lucretia James, Storage Technology, Inc., Louisville, Colorado

Kathy Collins Smith, American Institute of Banking, Denver, Colorado

Wade Murphree, Denver Institute of Technology, Colorado

Calvin Frazier, State Department of Education, Denver, Colorado

Robert Taylor, The Ohio State University, Columbus

John Peper, Jefferson County Schools, Lakewood, Colorado

Michael A. MacDowell, Joint Council on Economic Education, New York, New York

Larry Brown, 70001, Inc., Washington, D.C.

Robert Stewart, University of Missouri, Columbia

Gordon Dickinson, Colorado Community College and Vocational Education Board, Sterling

Karl Weiss, Northeastern University, Boston, Massachusetts

Donald Schwartz, University of Colorado, Colorado Springs

Patricia Brevik, Auraria Library and Media Center, Denver, Colorado

John Dromgoole, National Commission on Cooperative Education, Boston, Massachusetts

Faith Hamre, Littleton Public Schools, Ohio

Vernon Broussard, National Council on Vocational Education, Culver City, California

David Terry, Utah System of Higher Education, Salt Lake City

Georgia Van Adestine, Western Michigan University, Kalamazoo, Michigan

Gordon E. Heaton, Colorado Education Association, Aurora, Colorado

Young Jay Mulkey, American Institute for Character Education, San Antonio, Texas

George P. Rusteika, Far West Laboratory for Educational Research and Development, San Francisco, California

Gordon M. Ambach, State Education Department, Albany, New York
Donald Clark, National Association for Industry-Education Cooperation, Buffalo, New York
Jacqueline Danzberger, Youth-Work, Inc., Washington, D.C.
Charles Davis, Education Clinics, Inc., Seattle, Washington
Dennis A. Dirksen, San Diego State University, California
Ben Lawrence, National Center for Higher Education Management Systems, Boulder, Colorado
Bill Rosser and Jennie Sanchez, Chicano Education Project, Denver, Colorado
Sandra K. Squires, University of Nebraska, Omaha

Related Activities in the Denver Area
Site Visits
> Warren Occupational Technology Center, Golden
>> Byron Tucker, Principal
> Mountain Bell Education and Training Center, Lakewood
>> Fred Wells, Director
> Career Education Center, Denver
>> John Astuno, Principal
> Emily Griffith Opportunity School, Denver
>> Butch Thomas, Principal

Luncheon discussion with Robert Worthington, Assistant Secretary for Vocational and Adult Education, U.S. Department of Education, Washington, D.C.

Dinner discussion with Willard Wirtz, National Institute for Work and Learning, Washington, D.C., and Henry David, National Institute of Education, Washington, D.C.

Dinner with business, education, and community leaders
> Sponsored by the Education Commission of the States
> Chaired by Calvin Frazier, Commissioner of Education, Colorado

Education for the Gifted and Talented
James J. Gallagher, University of North Carolina, Chapel Hill
Marcel Kinsbourne, Eunice Kennedy Shriver Center, Waltham, Massachusetts
Joseph Renzulli, University of Connecticut, Storrs
David Feldman, Tufts University, Medford, Massachusetts

William Durden, Johns Hopkins University, Baltimore, Maryland
Connie Steele, Texas Technical University, Lubbock
Isa Kaftal Zimmerman, Lexington Public Schools, Massachusetts
Alexinia Baldwin, State University of New York, Albany

Arthur Pontarelli, Rhode Island State Department of Education, Providence
Armand E. Bastastini, Jr., Rhode Island State Legislature, Providence
William R. Holland, Narragansett School District, Rhode Island
Melissa Lawton, Bristol School District, Rhode Island
Rachel Christina, Bristol School District, Rhode Island
Catherine Valentino, North Kingstown School District, Rhode Island
Marie Friedel, National Foundation for Gifted and Creative Children, Providence, Rhode Island
Marsha R. Berger, Rhode Island Federation of Teachers, Providence
Sidney Rollins, Rhode Island College, Providence
David Laux, State Advocates for Gifted Education, Providence, Rhode Island
James A. Di Prete, Coventry High School, Rhode Island
Harold Raynolds, Maine State Department of Education, Augusta
June K. Goodman, Connecticut State Board of Education, Hartford
Mary Hunter Wolfe, Connecticut State Task Force on Gifted and Talented Education, Hartford
Paul Regnier, speaking on behalf of Gordon Ambach, State Education Department, Albany, New York
Benson Snyder, Massachusetts Institute of Technology, Cambridge, Massachusetts
June Cox, Sid Richardson Foundation, Fort Worth, Texas
Loretta L. Frissora, Needham Public Schools, Massachusetts, representing the National Education Association
Patricia O'Connell, Augusta, Maine, representing the Council of State Directors for Programs for the Gifted

Virginia Ehrlich, Astor Program Studies for Gifted, Suffern, New York
Gloria Duclos, University of Southern Maine, Portland
Anton Lysy, Londonderry School District, New Hampshire
Rhoda Spear, New Haven Schools, Connecticut
Judith Grunbaum, Southeastern Massachusetts University, North Dartmouth
Vincent Hawes, American Association of State Colleges and Universities, Washington, D.C.

Dorothy Moser, Mortar Board, Inc., Columbus, Ohio

Wendy Marcks, Chelmsford Association for Talented and Gifted, Massachusetts

James DeLisle, University of Connecticut, Storrs

Naomi Zymelman, Charles E. Smith Jewish Day School, Rockville, Maryland

Sherry Earle, Connecticut Association for the Gifted, Danbury

C. Grey Austin, University of Georgia, Athens

Sally Reis, Council for Exceptional Children, Talented and Gifted Division, Reston, Virginia

Betty T. Gilson, Brockton Public Schools, Massachusetts

Roberta McHardy, Louisiana Department of Education, Baton Rouge

Felicity Freund, Gifted Child Society, Oakland, New Jersey

Lydia Smith, Simmons College, Boston, Massachusetts

Betsy Buchbinder, Massachusetts Association for Advancement of Individual Potential, Milton

Artemis Kirk, Simmons College, Boston, Massachusetts, representing the Association of College and Research Libraries

---

Elizabeth F. Abbott, Governor's Program for Gifted and Talented, Gainesville, Florida

James Alvino, Gifted Child Newsletter, Sewell, New Jersey

Gordon M. Ambach, State Education Department, Albany, New York

Association of San Diego Educators for the Gifted and Talented, California

Philip J. Burke and Karen A. Verbeke, University of Maryland, College Park

Sheila Brown, Nebraska Department of Education, Lincoln

California Association for the Gifted, Downey

Carolyn M. Callahan, The Association for the Gifted

Anne B. Crabbe, Coe College, Cedar Rapids, Iowa

Roxanne H. Cramer, American Mensa, Arlington, Virginia

Neil Daniel, Texas Christian University, Fort Worth

Sue Ellen Duggan and Mary Lou Fernandes, Lackawanna City School District, New York

John F. Feldhusen, Purdue University, West Lafayette, Indiana

Frank F. Fowle, III, Clayton, Missouri

Joseph Harrington, College Academy, Stoughton, Massachusetts

Anne E. Impellizzeri, American Association for Gifted Children

Betty Johnson, Minnesota Council for the Gifted and Talented, Minneapolis

Nancy Kalajian, Sommerville, Massachusetts
John Lawson, Massachusetts Department of Education, Quincy
Barbara Lindsey, Southwest Iowans for Talented and Gifted, Council Bluffs
Diane Modest, Framingham Public Schools, Massachusetts
Jack L. Omond, Office for the Gifted, Port Elizabeth, South Africa
Arthur Purcell, Resource Policy Institute, Washington, D.C.
Annette Raphel, Milton Academy, Massachusetts
Susanne Richert, Educational Improvement Center, Sewell, New Jersey
Carl L. Riehm, Virginia State Department of Education, Richmond
Terry Ruby, Raynham Public Schools, Massachusetts
Barbara Moore Schuch, San Diego City Schools, California
Dorothy Sisk, University of South Florida, Tampa
Mercedes Smith, Gifted Association of Missouri, Springfield
Christopher L. Sny, Janesville Public Schools, Wisconsin
Julian C. Stanley, SMPY, Department of Psychology, Johns Hopkins University, Baltimore, Maryland
Jo Thomason and Frederick J. Weintraub, Council for Exceptional Children, Reston, Virginia
Jo Anne Welch, Mississippi Association for the Talented and Gifted

Related Activities in the Boston Area
Site Visits
      Buckingham, Brown and Nichols School, Cambridge
          Peter Gunness, Headmaster
      Brookline High School, Brookline
          Robert McCarthy, Headmaster

Secretary's Regional Representatives
The Secretary's Regional Representatives held their own conferences or hearings for educators in their regions in order to provide additional testimony to the Commission. In addition to these events, they also supported the hearings the Commission sponsored in their regions.

Region I, Wayne Roberts
Boston, Massachusetts
Forum on Effective Schools, September 16, 1982

Region II, Lorraine Colville
New York, New York
Forum on Excellence, October 21, 1982

Region III, Joseph Ambrosino
Philadelphia, Pennsylvania
Hearing/Conference on Cooperative Education, October 11, 1982

Region IV, Ted B. Freeman
Atlanta, Georgia
Public Meeting on Excellence in Education, October 22, 1982

Region V, Harold Wright
Chicago, Illinois
Excellence in Education: Preparation for the Transition to Higher
Education, October 6, 1982

Region VI, Scott Tuxhorn
Dallas, Texas
Public Hearing on Excellence in Education, October 4, 1982

Region VII, Cynthia A. Harris
Kansas City, Missouri
Rural and Small Schools Excellence, October 26, 1982

Region VIII, Tom Tancredo
Denver, Colorado
Conference on Excellence in Education, November 12-13, 1982

Region IX, Eugene Gonzales
San Francisco, California
The Teacher: Key to Excellence in the Classroom, October 18, 1982

Region X, George Hood
Seattle, Washington
Public Hearing, June 25, 1982, August 27, 1982
(Hearing Officer: Hyrum M. Smith)

Transcripts of the preceding hearings sponsored by and for the Commission will be available in the ERIC System.

In addition to these hearings sponsored by and for the Commission, Commission members participated in a series of site visits and a public hearing focusing on Excellence in Rural Education. These events took place on April 23-24, 1982, in Kentucky. The hearing was held at the University of Kentucky-Somerset Community College.

Appendix F: Other Presentations to the Commission

Adrienne Bailey, The College Board, New York, New York
Stephen Bailey, Harvard Graduate School of Education, Cambridge, Massachusetts
Irene Bandy, Ohio Department of Education, Columbus
Elias Blake, Clark College, Atlanta, Georgia
Lewis M. Branscomb, National Science Board, Washington, D.C.
David Burnett, University of Pennsylvania, Philadelphia
Lawrence Cremin, Teachers College, Columbia University, New York, New York
James V. Gaddy, New Rochelle High School, New York
John Goodlad, University of California, Los Angeles
Elaine Hairston, Ohio Board of Regents, Columbus
John Hurley, INA Corporation (Now CIGNA), Philadelphia, Pennsylvania
Edward Kelly, State University of New York at Albany
Robert McMillan, University of Rhode Island, Kingston
Edward Pellegrino, Georgetown Medical Center, Washington, D.C.
Francis Roberts, National Endowment for the Humanities, Washington, D.C.
David S. Seeley, Staten Island, New York
John Sprott, U.S. Department of State, Washington, D.C.
Carol Stoel, U.S. Department of Education, Washington, D.C.
Abraham Tannenbaum, Teachers College, Columbia University, New York, New York
Harold Tragash, Xerox Corporation, Stamford, Connecticut

Appendix G: Notable Programs

Institutions Which Submitted Profiles of Programs

With the assistance of a variety of organizations, the Commission conducted four searches for examples of notable programs and promising approaches to specific problems in American education. Our purpose was to understand better how schools, school districts, colleges, and other education organizations were defining and addressing these problems. Where the evidence was convincing, we also sought to learn what made successful programs work in different settings.

The Commission's procedure in these four searches was to solicit original profiles of these programs and approaches, profiles that would answer a number of key questions concerning their purpose, content, organization, impact, and transferability.

Evidence of program success was provided wholly by the institution submitting the profile. The Commission is, thus, in no position to validate these programs or to claim any of them to be "exemplary."

Over 200 schools, school districts, colleges, and other educational organizations responded to our solicitations. They sent in profiles and other descriptions of nearly 300 programs. Due to the specific problems on which we were seeking information (e.g., the transition from secondary to postsecondary education, the use of educational technology, mathematics education, cooperative educational ventures with business and industry), most of the respondents were postsecondary institutions. But many of the profiles submitted by colleges involved programs developed for or with elementary and/or secondary schools and are in operation in many school districts.

For their assistance in the efforts to identify and solicit this information, we are particularly grateful to the American Council on Education, the American Association for Higher Education, the American Association of State Colleges and Universities, the American Association of Community and Junior Colleges, the National Association of Secondary School Principals, the Academy for Educational Development, the Council on American Private Education, and the Fund for the Improvement of Postsecondary Education.

113

The following document will be available in the ERIC System sometime after July, 1983 (See Ordering Information):

Authors
Clifford Adelman
   National Institute of Education
   Washington, D.C.

Elaine Reuben
   Elaine Reuben Associates
   Washington, D.C.

Paper
"Notable Programs in American Postsecondary Education: Selected Analytical Abstracts"

Ordering Information

Additional copies of this study may be obtained from bookstores nationwide and from:

USA Research, Inc.
4380 SW Macadam Avenue
Portland, OR 97201-6406
telephone 503-274-6200
facsimile 503-274-6265

Copies of commissioned research papers are available from ERIC Document Reproduction Service, P.O. Box 190, Arlington, VA 22210, telephone 703-841-1212.